The Macintosh Way

G U Y   K A W A S A K I

Scott, Foresman and Company

Glenview, Illinois   London

The quotation on page 151 is excerpted from *Fred Astaire—His Friends Talk* by Sarah Giles. Copyright © 1988 by Sarah Giles. Reprinted by permission of Doubleday, a division of Bantam, Doubleday, Dell Publishing Group, Inc.

Library of Congress Cataloging-in-Publication Data
Kawasaki, Guy.
    The Macintosh way / Guy Kawasaki.

    Includes index.
    1. Apple Computer, Inc. Macintosh Division—History. 2. Macintosh (Computer)—Programming—Marketing—History. 3. Computer software—Marketing—History. 4. Micro-computers—Programming—Marketing—History. I. Title.
HD9696.C64A865   1989   89-10249
338.7'61004165'0973—dc20

  2 3 4 5 6 KPF 94 93 92 91 90 89

ISBN 0-673-46175-0

Scott, Foresman professional books are available for bulk sales at quantity discounts. For information, please contact Marketing Manager, Professional Books Group, Scott, Foresman and Company, 1900 East Lake Avenue, Glenview, IL 60025.

Table of Contents

A Brief History of Macintosh

1983 Year 1 Before Macintosh (B.M.)   **1984** Year 0

September	October	November	December	January	February
▲ Started working at Apple				▲ Introduction of Macintosh ("1984" Super Bowl commercial) 1/24/84	

March	April	May	June	July	August
	▲ 100,000 Macintoshes sold				

1985 Year 1 After Macintosh (A.M.)

September	October	November	December	January	February
▲ 512K Mac introduced	▲ Test Drive a Macintosh promotion			▲ Introduction of Macintosh Office (LaserWriter, Lemmings TV commercial) 1/23/85	

March	April	May	June	July	August
	▲ Macintosh XL laid to rest		▲ Layoffs and re-organization 6/14/85	▲ PageMaker ships, "desktop" becomes an adjective	

1986 Year 2 After Macintosh (A.M.)

September	October	November	December	January	February
Steve Jobs resigns from Apple				Introduction of the Macintosh Plus and LaserWriter Plus (no Super Bowl TV commercial)	

March	April	May	June	July	August
4th Dimension acquired by Apple			4th Dimension shown to Ed Esber		Apple Programmer's and Developer's Association (APDA) formed

1987 Year 3 After Macintosh (A.M.)

September	October	November	December	January	February
		Turned down for directorship 12/4/86	4th Dimension meeting with Ashton-Tate 12/12/86	Sculley tells Esber that Apple won't publish 4th Dimension. Esber tries to rearrange Gassée's anatomy.	

March		April		
Macintosh SE and Macintosh II introduced	Made director 4/1/87	Resigned from Apple 4/3/87	Last day at Apple 4/17/87	ACIUS starts 4/20/87

May	June	July	August	September
Macintosh II ships	4th Dimension ships			dBASE Mac ships

En Guise de Foreword

The Gentle Art of Verbal Self-Defense this book is not. *The Macintosh Way* is the take-no-prisoners guide to guerrilla marketing warfare in the personal computer software industry. I trust it will upset and delight the right people.

Guy Kawasaki speaks from a position of authority. His mission was equivalent to that of a Hollywood film producer's: "I have $10 million out of the $20 million budget for this movie with Robert Redford and Barbra Streisand. Will you invest one tenth of the total, a mere $2 million?" You may have nothing to start with except your belief that once you get enough people committed, you'll finally get the stars. This was Apple's and Guy's predicament—how do you convince the world of software developers it is a good idea to invest their energy into writing software for a computer with no installed base?

The rest is another proof that a few things at Apple (besides some of its founders and executives) defy common sense. Macintosh now enjoys abundant software—the best there is in the business. This is to the credit of the designers of the Macintosh, of the creative and patient software developers, and of Guy Kawasaki and his fellow evangelists.

Guy himself is quite an improbable combination. The son of two delightful and proud Japanese Americans, he speaks the Yiddish he learned in the jewelry business and is an inveterate francophile, a dedicated husband, and a trustworthy friend. The last two items sound a little bit corny and conventional?

Well, read on and enjoy a not so corny and conventional paean to great times, feisty people, and smart ways. And some tart inside anecdotes too.

Jean-Louis Gassée
President, Apple
Products

Preface

This book is about doing the right thing and doing things right. It is meant for dreamers, revolutionaries, Macintosh aficionados, and all the people who want to learn about the Macintosh Way. It is aimed at the inner circle, and it is not meant to appeal to the largest possible audience or the lowest common denominator.

The book is divided into three parts:

▶ Part I is an introduction to the Macintosh Way. It covers the history of Macintosh and provides an analysis of what the Macintosh phenomenon means.

▶ Part II is called "Doing the Right Thing." It covers the work environment, products, marketing, and customer support; these are the foundations of a great company.

▶ Part III is called "Doing Things Right." It covers the details of running a business right, such as evangelism, distribution, user groups, trade shows, PR, demos, motherships, competition, presentations, and of course, dating and marriage.

This is not a gentle book—it celebrates passion, competition, excellence, and hard work. The basic premise is that David can defeat Goliath, that a teenager can fly into Red Square, and that an ex-jewelry schlepper from Hawaii can eat paté with a French philosopher at Jacques Cagna in Paris.

I used to work at Apple so I have many nostalgic and mixed feelings about the place. In the book I take some shots at Apple because I believe in the Macintosh Uncertainty Principle—you must observe the foibles of Apple to change it.

However, I also believe that most people who criticize Apple couldn't possibly run it any better. Fundamentally, Apple is a great company with great employees and great products. Most of Apple's harshest critics couldn't run a lemonade stand on a hot day and don't deserve to.

I will unveil to you the genetic code of the Macintosh Way of doing business. For what it's worth, I release my ideas, thoughts, and methods in this book for you to use. Let us not compete on the knowledge of strategies and tactics. Let us compete on execution.

Merci

I used to think that writing a book was a solitary endeavor. It's not. Like any product, a book requires a team of testers, beta sites, and supporters, and I would like to acknowledge the people who helped me.

Marylène Delbourg-Delphis. She is a female, French Steve Jobs. She pushed me higher than I ever thought I could go. One should be so lucky to have a mentor like her. I wish she would stop smoking.

David Brandt, Kyle Mashima and Terri Lonier. David, Kyle, and Terri helped make my incomplete thoughts into a book. Without their assistance, I'm afraid of what this book would have been.

Susie Hammond, Denise Caruso, Dave Winer, Jean-Louis Gassée, Don "Perignon" Crabb, Steve Scheier, Dan Farber, Scott Knaster, Henry Norr, Jerry Borrell, Laurie Flynn, Sue Jacoby, Duke Kawasaki, Mitch Stein, Joanna Hoffman, Steve Bobker, Pauline Mashima, Dave Graebel, Alain Rossmann, Robert Wiggins, and Tony Oppenheim. They were my beta testers. Each tweaked the book in his or her own special way.

Jo Ann Vandervennet and Karen Seale. Jo Ann and Karen manage Jean-Louis. They gave me access to him to help me finish this book in a timely manner. I guess it's who you know at Apple.

Will Mayall, Kathryn Henkens, Todd Carper, Bruce Finch, Mark Vernon, A.J. Jennings, Ron Dell'Aquila, Dave Terry, and Jaime

ix

Montemayor. This is the ACIUS team who politely read draft after draft of the book and helped make it better. They also didn't hesitate to point out where the book and ACIUS reality diverged.

Stephen Roth. Stephen Roth was the editor and producer of the book. If you find an editor who understands what you are trying to do, brings the best out of you, and doesn't botch up your work, "marry" him as fast as you can.

Mei-Ying Dell'Aquila. Mei-Ying created the analog drawings for the book. The samurai and chicken man and most of the graphics were her ideas. I tried to keep her so busy that she didn't have time to work on HyperCard stacks.

Amy Davis. Amy Davis is the editor at Scott, Foresman who acquired this book contrary to traditional book publishing wisdom, which said, "There are two kinds of books: *How to Use 1-2-3* and *How to be a Manager.* Yours is neither. Sorry Mr. Kawasaki." She did the right thing, IMHO.[1]

Olav Martin Kvern. Ole (that's pronounced O-lee) designed and helped to produce the book, and created most of the electronic art. He also contributed a joke or two.

Beth Kawasaki. Thanks and love to my wife. She puts up with immeasurable amounts of grief being married to me, and she still loves me. If you find a woman who is smart, funny, honest, beautiful, and loves you, marry her as fast as you can. She's not a bad content editor, either.

Finally, I'd like to thank the developers who believed in Macintosh from the beginning, stuck with it, made it great, and were a pleasure to work with when I was at Apple.

CE Software	West Des Moines, Iowa
Consulair	Ketchum, Idaho
Creative Solutions	Rockville, Maryland
Douglas Electronics	San Leandro, California
Living Videotext	Mountain View, California
Magic Software	Bellevue, Nebraska
Magnus Corporation	Mukilteo, Washington

---

1. IMHO is online talk for "in my humble opinion."

Mainstay	Agoura Hills, California
Megahaus	San Diego, California
National Instruments	Austin, Texas
Odesta Corporation	Northbrook, Illinois
ProVUE Development	Huntington Beach, California
Silicon Beach Software	San Diego, California
Softview, Inc.	Camarillo, California
Spectrum Digital Systems	Madison, Wisconsin
Solutions International	Williston, Vermont
Survivor Software	Los Angeles, California
T/Maker Company	Mountain View, California
Telos Corporation	Santa Monica, California
TML Systems	Jacksonville, Florida
VAMP, Inc.	Los Angeles, California
Working Software	Santa Cruz, California

May they keep the spirit alive.

Guy Kawasaki

History

Part 1

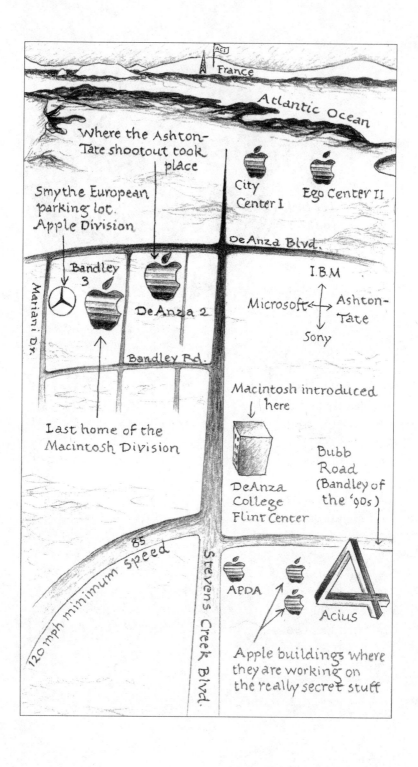

First Blood

The higher a monkey climbs, the more
you can see of his behind.
General "Vinegar
Joe" Stilwell

Inside the Apple Board Room

"If Guy leaves, we all leave," replied Bill Campbell, the executive vice-president of sales and marketing of Apple. Luther Nussbaum, the president of Ashton-Tate, had suggested that I leave the room because Ashton-Tate was going to provide an update about dBASE Mac, their Macintosh database. Campbell spoke very calmly and quietly yet everyone in the room knew that Ashton-Tate had to back down. Nussbaum wanted me to leave the room because I was the primary supporter of an Apple database project called "Silver Surfer"[1] that would compete with his product.

It was December 18, 1986, and a large group of Apple and Ashton-Tate executives had gathered in Apple's board room to discuss the Silver Surfer project. Bill Campbell, John Sculley, Del Yocam, Jean-Louis Gassée, and I represented Apple. Ed Esber, Luther Nussbaum, Roy Folk, and Mike Stone represented Ashton-Tate. I was the person in charge of the software published by Apple and the relationship between Apple and its developers, and I had spent about two hours explaining why Apple needed to publish its own database.

---

1. 4th Dimension was code-named "Silver Surfer" because Silver Surfer is one of the favorite comic book characters of the author of 4th Dimension, Laurent Ribardière.

Background—The Silver Surfer Project

At the time, Macintosh had a good selection of desktop[1] publishing, graphics, word processing, and spreadsheet software but not high-end relational databases, and this shortcoming prevented Macintosh from entering the mainstream of business

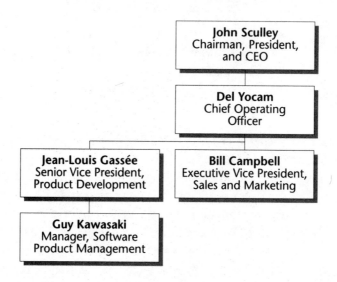

The Apple Team

computing. As a software evangelist,[2] I had spent almost two years unsuccessfully trying to convince developers, including Ashton-Tate, to create such a product, and it was time for Apple to take control of its own fate.

Two years before the meeting, the world was very different. Macintosh was not selling well. It was not perceived as a powerful computer. Most business people scoffed at it as a "cute,

---

1. Desktop is an adjective that Aldus originally applied to "publishing" because a Macintosh and LaserWriter enabled people to bring the power of expensive electronic composition to their desks. Desktop used to be a noun. Now it is an adjective that Apple applies to every market because it worked once.

2. Software evangelism is a term coined by Mike Murray of the Macintosh Division. It meant using fervor and zeal (but never money) to convince software developers to create products for a computer with no installed base, 128K of RAM, no hard disk, no documentation, and no technical support, made by a flaky company that IBM was about to snuff out.

graphics toy." A lot of people didn't even think that Apple would survive. Many large developers doubted that Macintosh would succeed and were skeptical that our graphics toy could support a high-end relational database.

During a trip to France in 1985, Steve Jobs saw a product

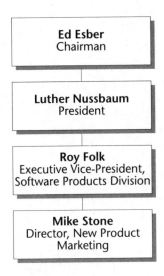

The Ashton-Tate Team

called 4th Dimension and encouraged the programmer, Laurent Ribardière, and his partner, Marylène Delbourg-Delphis, to create an American version. Steve told them to show it to me and Alain Rossmann because we were Apple's software evangelists in Cupertino and might be able to help them find an American publisher. When Alain saw it in the Fall of 1985, he was thrilled by the prospect that Macintosh would have a high-end, graphic database. It was a product that would help change the perception that Macintosh was not powerful.

Alain's first reaction was to matchmake Laurent and Marylène with American companies like Microsoft and Ashton-Tate because we preferred not to acquire products that would compete with our developers. Most American companies, however, weren't interested in a Macintosh database because of poor

Macintosh sales at the time. Instead of letting 4th Dimension remain a Europe-only product, Alain and I decided to acquire it for Apple because we both believed that 4th Dimension was a great product. It became the Silver Surfer project.

Alain and I believed that Apple could not wait for Ashton-Tate and other MS-DOS database companies to commit to Macintosh—it was not until September, 1987 that Ashton-Tate finally shipped dBASE Mac. The inside story is that Bill Campbell had to promise Ashton-Tate $500,000 in co-marketing funds to finish dBASE Mac. When Ashton-Tate finally shipped, a year later than promised to Apple, it still had the gall to demand the $500,000. I think Apple eventually settled the matter by giving Ashton-Tate some Macintosh IIs. dBASE Mac was the best database that Macintosh IIs could buy.

Back to the Board Room

Ashton-Tate's Mike Stone was about to begin his presentation when Nussbaum made the suggestion that I leave. I remained in the meeting, and Stone's dBASE Mac update made all of three points—beta[1] sites were seeded, they were generally happy, and they were concerned with performance. For this, Nussbaum wanted me to leave the room. His suggestion was ludicrous. I probably knew more about the state of dBASE Mac than Nussbaum or Esber because the technical support group that helped Ashton-Tate worked for me. Apple engineers like Jim Friedlander constantly visited Ashton-Tate to give them house-call care.

After Stone's presentation, Sculley, Yocam, Gassée, Campbell, Esber, Folk, and Nussbaum adjourned for a private meeting while the worker bees waited in Apple's board room. Esber told Sculley, Yocam, and Gassée that he was not officially informed of 4th Dimension until a few weeks before the meeting. That

---

1. Beta sites are people who get beta or prerelease copies of software so that they can feel important. The term "beta" is an abbreviation for the phrase "beta than nothing," which is exactly what beta software is. Software companies like to give beta sites beta software because they think it prevents them from buying the shipping versions of their competitor's products. When a company tells you a ship date for beta software, you had better be able to read between the lies.

wasn't true. Alain told Mike Stone and Roy Folk before he left Apple in July, 1986. I told Esber in his office in June, 1986 when Alain and I visited Ashton-Tate to make a Macintosh presentation. Esber complained bitterly to Sculley, Yocam, and Gassée about my competency and the handling of 4th Dimension. He tried to ruin my reputation and my career at Apple. He drew first blood.

Post Meeting Blues

After the meeting Jean-Louis told me that Esber and Nussbaum wanted Apple to give 4th Dimension to Ashton-Tate so that they could "combine" 4th Dimension and dBASE Mac. The idea of combining the two products was the most profound example of not understanding Macintosh software development that I'd ever seen. Macintosh software products are intellectual and artistic works. Like painting, sculpture, or music, they cannot be combined and remain either intellectual or artistic.

After the meeting, I was instructed to provide Ashton-Tate with a prerelease copy of 4th Dimension. Giving Ashton-Tate a copy would have been unfair to Laurent and Marylène. 4th Dimension was their property, and we had no right to give it to a company like Ashton-Tate who would probably kill it. I couldn't refuse, but I could subvert. Kyle Mashima, the manager of Apple-labeled software, and I searched for and found a way to avoid giving Ashton-Tate a copy. We had previously executed a mutual nondisclosure agreement[1] with Laurent and Marylène. We "couldn't" legally give Ashton-Tate a prerelease copy, and they never got one.

Ashton-Tate's behavior towards 4th Dimension, Macintosh, and Apple reminded me of bald men who take their last wisps of hair and comb them unnaturally across their scalps to cover their heads. In the process they only bring more attention to their baldness. Ashton-Tate's baldness was a lack of allegiance to Macintosh, lack of knowledge about what was going on in their own company, and lack of understanding of Macintosh database

---

1. A mutual nondisclosure agreement means that you and Apple agree not to divulge each other's secrets. In practice, it means that Apple can leak all it wants, and you can't do anything about it.

needs. Ashton-Tate didn't drink from the Macintosh well; it gargled.

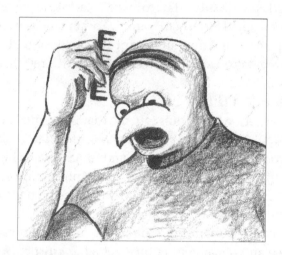

Au Revoir, Apple

Two weeks before the meeting with Ashton-Tate, I was denied a directorship at Apple because I had failed to manage Apple's relationship with Ashton-Tate and Microsoft. This was the Ashton-Tate that couldn't finish dBASE Mac, and the Microsoft that Apple would sue for copyright violation. Frankly, I didn't want to manage Apple's alliance[1] with these companies because they did business by holding a gun to Apple's head. I began to think that it was time to leave Apple when the fleas started wagging the dog.

In February, 1987, two months after the Ashton-Tate meeting, John Sculley told Ed Esber at Esther Dyson's computer conference[2] in Phoenix, Arizona that Apple would not compete with Ashton-Tate by publishing 4th Dimension.

Jean-Louis' assessment of Ashton-Tate's victory was

---

1. "Alliance, n: in international politics, the union of two thieves who have their hands so deeply inserted into each other's pockets that they cannot safely plunder a third." —Ambrose Bierce

2. Esther Dyson's computer conference is an annual gathering where computer industry people pay $1,000 to listen to other computer industry people brag about how smart they are and to talk to people they can't stand seeing outside of the conference.

$\bullet$

December 4, 1986

TO: Guy Kawasaki

FROM: Del Yocam

SUBJECT: <u>**Review Commentary**</u>

Guy, I've read Jean-Louis' assessment of your performance during this review period. Since you also worked for me during this time I wanted to add some of my thoughts.

You have much to be proud of in the reputation you've established as a premier evangelist. This has long been a strength of yours and it is one from which Apple has greatly benefitted . I now look to you for a broader scope of responsibility. In my mind you've always championed "the little guy" in the developer community. Those developers have made a great difference to our success and I want Apple to continue to be the personal computer company they look to first. But, I believe the Product Management Software Manager needs to have established the same reputation with the "big guys", most notably Microsoft and Ashton-Tate. In my most recent dealing with these organizations I've had to depend on Jean-Louis to be sure that Apple's relationship with these leaders was at a level which made me comfortable. When I think about who the "program manager" for Apple's relationship with Microsoft and Ashton-Tate is, I do not have the confidence that you've made this a priority. I therefore look to Jean-Louis.

Guy, I think you are a great asset to Apple. But before I can support a move in which you would join my senior management team, I need to be more comfortable with your relationship with Apple's largest third party software developers. I am willing to work with you and Jean-Louis to make this happen because both of us believe in your potential.

DWY/sg

"sometimes you get what you ask for, and it's not what you really want" because the Silver Surfer affair catalyzed the formation of both Claris[1] and ACIUS.[2] In effect, Ashton-Tate created two new competitors in the Macintosh market by terrorizing Apple: ACIUS was formed to bring 4th Dimension to

---

1. Claris is Latin for "clarity." I have a real affinity for Claris because it was one of the best ideas I ever had.

2. ACIUS stands for "Apple Computer, Inc. Unshipped Software." Just kidding. The name of our French founding company is Analyses Conseils Informations ("ACI") so we are ACI in the US.

market in America, and Claris was spun off from Apple with the Apple-labeled software to reduce competition between Apple and its developers. I think that John and Jean-Louis secretly hoped it would come out this way, and two more Macintosh software companies would be formed.

On April 1, 1987 (an appropriate date), at the Apple Developers' Conference, Jean-Louis promoted me to director of software product management. It was too late for Apple to keep me, but I've always appreciated the fact that Jean-Louis got me a directorship. That night I gave my last speech as an Apple employee at the Developers' Conference dinner. Some of the audience knew that I was leaving because a long-term Apple employee wouldn't dare say what I did.

I began with a roll call of people like Bill Gates, the chairman of Microsoft, and Jim Manzi, the president of Lotus, because I knew they weren't at our conference. They were at an IBM Windows[1] conference instead. I also read a list of people who were at our conference, such as Mitch Stein of Spectrum Digital Systems, Mary Evslin of Solutions International, Charlie Jackson of Silicon Beach Software, and Sue Morgan of SoftView, because they were the presidents of little companies who believed in Macintosh from the start. It was not a subtle speech, and I hoped that word would get back to the MS-DOS boys.

On April 3, 1987 I sent my resignation in a Federal Express package to Jean-Louis in France. It was a desktop resignation letter—multiple columns, integrated graphics, and bar charts. I even had it framed for Jean-Louis. On April 17, I was out of Apple. On April 20, ACIUS was born.

The Macintosh Way

For me, it was sad to see a once-fanatical company like Apple successfully threatened by an MS-DOS developer—and an MS-DOS developer with an extraordinarily ordinary product at that. A little piece of me died because of the Silver Surfer affair.

---

1. Windows is an operating environment that attempts to turn a real computer into a cute, graphics toy. It is also the subject of a lawsuit between Apple and Microsoft.

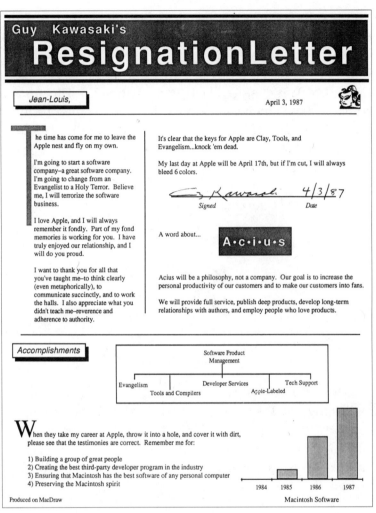

Guy Kawasaki's
ResignationLetter

Jean-Louis,

April 3, 1987

The time has come for me to leave the Apple nest and fly on my own.

I'm going to start a software company–a great software company. I'm going to change from an Evangelist to a Holy Terror. Believe me, I will terrorize the software business.

I love Apple, and I will always remember it fondly. Part of my fond memories is working for you. I have truly enjoyed our relationship, and I will do you proud.

I want to thank you for all that you've taught me–to think clearly (even metaphorically), to communicate succinctly, and to work the halls. I also appreciate what you didn't teach me–reverence and adherence to authority.

It's clear that the keys for Apple are Clay, Tools, and Evangelism...knock 'em dead.

My last day at Apple will be April 17th, but if I'm cut, I will always bleed 6 colors.

Signed ___Kawasaki___   4/3/87 *Date*

A word about...

A•c•i•u•s

Acius will be a philosophy, not a company. Our goal is to increase the personal productivity of our customers and to make our customers into fans.

We will provide full service, publish deep products, develop long-term relationships with authors, and employ people who love products.

Accomplishments

Software Product Management

Evangelism | Developer Services | Tech Support
Tools and Compilers | Apple-Labeled

When they take my career at Apple, throw it into a hole, and cover it with dirt, please see that the testimonies are correct. Remember me for:

1) Building a group of great people
2) Creating the best third-party developer program in the industry
3) Ensuring that Macintosh has the best software of any personal computer
4) Preserving the Macintosh spirit

1984   1985   1986   1987

Produced on MacDraw

Macintosh Software

Ashton-Tate did the wrong thing (an ordinary product) the wrong way (by threatening Apple) at the wrong time (two years too late). If Ashton-Tate had believed in Macintosh and created a great database, we would not have acquired 4th Dimension.

There is a better way of doing business—it's called the Macintosh Way.

The Macintosh Way of doing business is rooted in the 1940s when Hewlett-Packard established a model for the high-tech industries of Silicon Valley. The H-P Way meant giving people the opportunity to do a good job, consensus decision-making, and egalitarian organizational structures. Even the trappings of autocratic management disappeared because open cubicles and workbenches replaced closed, corner offices.

In the 1980s Apple grabbed the baton from H-P. This upstart, arrogant, and vibrant company maintained the informality of the H-P Way and added its own elements of flashy products, splashy marketing, and reality distortion. This was the Apple Way. Somewhere along the line, however, another change took place, and the baton passed from Apple, the company, to Macintosh, the computer.

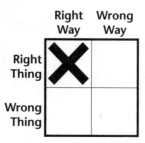

The Macintosh Way of doing business means doing the right thing and doing things right. It combines the informality of the H-P Way and the flair of the Apple Way with an idealistic faith in employees, customers, and products. It is a way of doing business for people who are foolish or brave enough to try to make a difference in a world of mediocrity.

Doing the Right Thing

The first part of the Macintosh Way is doing the right thing. It means focusing on the four essential tasks of a company: creating the work environment, developing products, supporting customers, and implementing marketing.

▶ The right work environment is created by passion and sustains action, risk-taking, and fun. The president or CEO of a company determines the quality of the work environment. A Yiddish saying sums it up, albeit negatively: "When the fish gets rotten, the head stinks first." Assuming your head isn't rotten, the next steps are to hire the right people and give them the freedom to do their jobs, because people are the most important assets of a company.

▶ The right products reward their owners; they are deep, indulgent, complete, and elegant. Canon EOS 35mm cameras are deep—they appeal to parents and professionals. Macintoshes are indulgent—you could buy an IBM PC clone, but it doesn't make you feel good (or guilty). WAMMs are complete—they are stereo speakers that the manufacturer comes to your home to install. *The Macintosh Bible* is another good example of a complete product; it's a book that comes with two free upgrades. Acura Legend Coupes are elegant— for half the price of a Mercedes, you can have a better car.

▶ The right customer support concentrates on the customer, not the corporate policy book or quarterly bottom line. The best example of the right customer support is a department store chain called Nordstrom. If every high-technology company aspired to be the Nordstrom of their market, it would be a better world. Nordstrom has fans, not customers, because it provides the right support.

▶ The right marketing communicates the benefits of technology by getting the right information into the hands of the right people. It is not dependent on expensive and impressive advertising campaigns or slick PR. It is the marketing of technology, not the technology of marketing. If you believe that your customers are intelligent, it's a matter of finding them and providing them with accurate, in-depth information. They'll make the right decisions.

Doing Things Right

The second part of the Macintosh Way is doing things right. It means paying attention to the details of running a business and building success brick by brick. It's not always necessary or glamorous to do things right, but Macintosh Way companies do them instinctively. For example:

▸ Evangelism is sales done right. It is the sharing of your dream with the marketplace and the making of history with your customer. Evangelism is the purest form of sales. A Macintosh Way company doesn't sell; it evangelizes.

▸ Giving information and support to user groups is word-of-mouth advertising done right. User groups are a medium like print or television, but you can't buy them. You have to earn them.

▸ Demos are sales presentations done right. Demos show customers *why* they should buy a product because they show *how* the product can increase their creativity and productivity.

Doing the right thing and doing things right are the two components of the Macintosh Way. Now let's review the history of Macintosh to build a foundation for understanding and implementing the Macintosh Way. Then we'll move on to discussing doing the right thing and doing things right.

Macintosh Days

Q. How many Macintosh Division employ-
ees do you need to change a light bulb?
A. One. He holds the light bulb up and lets
the universe revolve around him.

The employees of the
Apple II Division

Back to the Future

Macintosh is an example of how a person can get disgusted with mediocrity, do the right thing, and achieve extraordinary success. Essentially, Steve Jobs couldn't stand existing personal computers, did his own thing, and found (to his relief) that others agreed with him. In retrospect he was a visionary, but when he was creating Macintosh, his actions were natural and obvious to him.

Mediocrity—the antagonist—was IBM and MS-DOS. They stood for a status quo that few people noticed and most saw no reason to change. Steve challenged the status quo and put something into motion that grew larger than anyone envisioned. Macintosh started as a computer. It became a cult. Then a phenomenon. Then a standard. Now it is a way of doing business.

The development and introduction of Macintosh provides many examples of doing the right thing and doing things right. The history of Macintosh is conveniently documented elsewhere,[1] so I will provide the perspective of someone in the Macintosh Division. Admittedly, I was captured by the Macintosh phenomenon even as I was helping to create it.

---

1. Check out *The Journey is the Reward* by Jeffrey Young and *Odyssey* by John Sculley.

Introduction—1984

On January 23, 1984, Apple ran a teaser ad during the Super Bowl called "1984." It depicted a young, athletic woman disrupting a Big Brother rally. The introduction of Macintosh, the ad predicted, would mean that "1984 won't be like 1984."

The next day Steve Jobs, as only Steve Jobs could, unveiled Macintosh to 2,000 rabid Apple employees, shareholders, and fans at the Flint Center of DeAnza College in Cupertino. Steve even decided that Macintosh would be the first computer to introduce itself with digitized speech. Macintosh's first words were:

Hello, I am Macintosh. It sure is great to get out of that bag. Unaccustomed as I am to public speaking, I'd like to share with you a thought that occurred to me the first time I met an IBM mainframe. Never trust a computer you can't lift. Right now I'd like to introduce a man who has been like a father to me, Steve Jobs.

The Macintosh Division had a seating area reserved in the front of the auditorium. I'll never forget the special feeling of being able to sit there with the people who created Macintosh like Brian Howard, Bill Atkinson, Andy Hertzfeld, Burrell Smith, Joanna Hoffman, Steve Capps, and Bruce Horn. I'll also never forget the thrill of seeing my name on the screen when each Macintosh Division employee was listed in slides at the end of the presentation.

The Macintosh Division

Every story you heard about the Macintosh Division is true. We were the hand-picked children of Steve Jobs. The industry joke was, "What is the difference between Apple and the Cub Scouts?" The answer: "The Cub Scouts have adult supervision." It was like playing pinball only you were the ball.

On Thursdays and Fridays, masseuses came into our building, Bandley 3, and gave us massages at our desks. There was a Bösendorfer grand piano in the atrium of our building. It went along with $10,000 speakers and a CD player (back when CD players were still exotic).

Unlike any other part of Apple, the Macintosh Division flew first class if the trip was more than three hours long. I interpreted the three hours to start from the time I left my apartment, so I flew first class everywhere. We had unlimited supplies of freshly squeezed orange juice. Not the kind made from concentrate—this stuff cost $1.50 a bottle. There were Ansel Adams originals in the lobby of Bandley 3.

Steve kept his BMW motorcycle near the lobby, though I never saw him ride it. He regarded the motorcycle as "living art"—not a means of transportation. We contemplated installing a washer and dryer in the building so we could do our laundry while we worked. We even thought about building a sushi bar so we wouldn't have to go out for lunch.

Every member of the Macintosh Division who started before the end of July, 1983 was given a Macintosh shortly after the introduction. The Macintosh bore a personalized name plate that said, "In appreciation" and the employee's name. I started in September but got one anyway. Cary Clark, the technical support engineer who started after me and single-handedly helped 100 developers finish their software, got one too.

The Macintosh Dream

The Macintosh Division shared a dream, the Macintosh Dream, of changing the world by bringing computers to more people so that they could improve their personal creativity and enrich their lives. We all thought we were going to change the world with our little computer, and we worked 90 hours a week to do it. We drank six-color[1] Kool Aid every day.

A common misinterpretation of the excesses of the Macintosh Division is that the special treatment motivated us. Nothing could be further from the truth. Steve motivated us. He wielded a unique ability to make you feel like a god or like a bozo. (In Steve's eyes, there are only two kinds of people.) The excesses—fresh orange juice, massages, and flying first class—merely reinforced the importance of our mission.

Exercise

Give the employees of your company fresh orange juice. Buy a grand piano for your foyer. Let them fly first class. Give them massages every Friday afternoon.

Did they create a Macintosh?

Working for Steve was a terrifying and addictive experience. He would tell you that your work, your ideas, and sometimes your existence were worthless right to your face, right in front of everyone. Watching him crucify someone scared you into working incredibly long hours.

Working for Steve was also ecstasy. Once in a while he would tell you that you were great, and that made it all worth it. Watching him sanctify someone motivated you to exceed your capabilities. It wasn't exactly Theory Z, but it did produce Macintosh. We would have worked in the Macintosh Division even if he'd given us Tang.

---

1. "Six-color" refers to the six-color Apple logo. People who love Apple see six-color sunsets, eat six-color ice cream, and bleed in six colors.

Exercise

It may be said of men in general that they are ungrateful and fickle, dissemblers, avoiders of danger, and greedy of gain. So long as you shower benefits upon them, they are all yours; they offer you their blood, their substance, their lives and their children, provided the necessity for it is far off; but when near at hand, they revolt.

The Prince
Machiavelli

Why was Machiavelli wrong?

A. *He didn't give stock options to his employees.*

B. *The market for IPOs[1] was poor at the time.*

C. *The capital gains tax in Italy was too high.*

D. *He never met Steve Jobs.*

Steve's idea of Management By Wandering Around (MBWA) was to go up to a person and say, "I think Guy is a bozo. What do you think?" If you agreed, he'd go on to the next person and would say, "I think Guy is a bozo. Mike agrees with me. What do you think?"

If you disagreed and said that Guy was great, Steve would go to the next person and say, "I think Guy is great. Mike does too. What do you think?" It wasn't exactly what Tom Peters would prescribe as a management feedback process.

---

1. Most people think that IPO stands for Initial Public Offering. Really it stands for Initial Premature Offering. An IPO typically occurs when the founders of a company realize that they had better cash out because they won't ship a new product for several years. Usually it's premature because the company and its products are untested, but there's a sucker for everything. As a venture capitalist once said, "Do what makes money, and the fun will come."

We were totally convinced, though, that we were doing the right thing. George Crow, a hardware engineer, and Bob Belleville, director of engineering, were so convinced that they risked their careers by subverting Steve. They believed that the right disk drive to use in Macintoshes was a 3 1/2-inch Sony drive and continued to work with Sony despite Steve's decision to use an alternate manufacturer called Alps. George and Larry Kenyon once hid the Sony disk drive engineer ("a little Japanese guy" according to Andy Hertzfeld)[1] in a closet when Steve popped into the lab at an unexpected time. (Right thing, right way.)

Test Drive a Macintosh

We were having a great time, but Macintosh wasn't selling that well. The Apple II was paying our way. Although 250,000 Macintoshes were sold in the first year, we forecast total first-year sales of 425,000 units and monthly run rates of 40,000–65,000 by the end of 1984. Also, the university market accounted for about 35 percent of sales, and developers bought another ten percent. Business clearly did not accept a 128K Macintosh with no software as an alternative to the IBM PC. It took four years—until 1988—to achieve the 1984 sales forecasts.

In the fall of 1984, we introduced a marketing promotion called "Test Drive a Macintosh" to improve sales. This promotion, conceived by Mike Murray, enabled Apple dealers to loan Macintoshes to customers for a test drive. In splendid Macintosh arrogance, we believed that Macintosh would seduce customers overnight. It was a good idea, but the timing was all wrong because dealers didn't want the hassle of administering the loaner units during the busy Christmas season. (Right thing, wrong way.)

Looking back on 1984, the amazing thing was not our optimistic projection, but that we were able to sell 250,000 units of a 128K computer with no software and no hard disk. If history is recorded correctly, Mike Murray and other Macintosh

1. Andy Hertzfeld is a Macintosh software wizard and the purest form of the Macintosh dream.

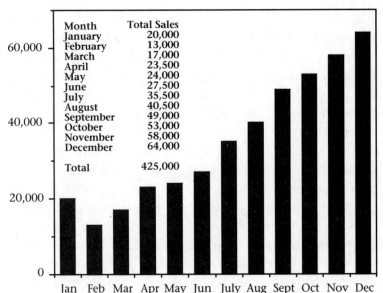

Month	Total Sales
January	20,000
February	13,000
March	17,000
April	23,500
May	24,000
June	27,500
July	35,500
August	40,500
September	49,000
October	53,000
November	58,000
December	64,000
Total	425,000

Original 1984 sales forecast from the Macintosh PIP (Product Introduction Plan),[1] November 7, 1983.

Division zealots like Joanna Hoffman, Barbara Koalkin, Steve Scheier, and John Rizzo will be remembered as people who changed personal computing forever with innovative ideas like Test Drive a Macintosh. Within six months of the introduction, the whole world knew about this easy-to-use computer with a graphic interface called Macintosh.

Exercise

Ask anyone from the Macintosh Division if they would do it all over again.

The Macintosh Office

During the 1985 Super Bowl, Apple ran another commercial. This one was called "Lemmings." The commercial antagonized

---

1. A Product Introduction Plan or PIP is a document that is circulated throughout Apple to ensure that everyone approves of a product introduction. In practice, it adds two months to the delivery of a product because no one is around to sign it. Also, no one reads it—everyone just sees who else signed it and signs it too.

many business people because it portrayed them as lemmings jumping off a cliff unless they "looked into the Macintosh Office." Rather than stunning the audience like "1984," it displayed Apple's self-delusions to millions of viewers. The commercial bombed, but the 49ers won and everyone at the Super Bowl in the Stanford Stadium got to keep an Apple seat cushion. Two out of three ain't bad.

The Macintosh Office was our vision of business people working in small groups of 5 to 25 people. It was made up of four primary components: Macintoshes, the AppleTalk network, peripherals like laser printers, and productivity applications. These "workgroups," as we called them, would be able to work more productively by sharing information and resources when tied together by a network. Until then, workgroup communication usually involved "SneakerNet"—carrying diskettes to each other on foot.

The problem with the Macintosh Office was that it was missing a fileserver—a device that acts something like a traffic cop and a shared storage device for a network. Early prototypes[1] were shown, but the fileserver was not even close to being completed. Because of this, Jean-Louis Gassée, then general manager of Apple France, refused to introduce the Macintosh Office in France. In his words, it was the "Macintosh Orifice." Apple didn't ship a fileserver until 1987.

The LaserWriter was the best part of the Macintosh Office. More than any other piece of hardware, it showed the distinct advantage of owning a Macintosh, and it saved Macintosh and enabled Apple to reemerge from 1985. Everyone takes the LaserWriter for granted today, but most of Apple fought against its creation. Many people, myself included, thought it was nuts to design a $7,000 printer—a Lisa[2] without a monitor if you will.

---

1. A prototype is a new piece of hardware or software that hasn't been officially released to the marketplace. Typically, it is a 10–20 percent improvement over the existing model with a 30–40 percent price increase. Often prototypes are sold as "version 1.0" to enable a broader population to pay for the privilege of testing the product.

2. A Lisa is a computer that was sold by Apple from 1983 to 1985. It represented much of the technology that eventually appeared in Macintosh, such as a one-

Bob Belleville championed the LaserWriter. He designed laser printers for Xerox and knew John Warnock, the creator of the PostScript[1] page description language and one of the founders of Adobe Systems. Though Apple marketing and the market demanded a daisy-wheel printer (the status quo thing), he pursued a laser printer for the rest of us. Bob, Steve, and Burrell Smith finished the LaserWriter despite strong resistance from all levels of Apple. (Right thing, right way.) Ironically, most of Apple fought against the very thing that probably saved it.

Exercise

Connect a daisy-wheel printer to a Macintosh. Create a newsletter with PageMaker.[2] Print the newsletter.

In June, 1985 Apple was ripped up and changed from a product division structure (Macintosh, Apple II) to a functional organization (development, marketing, and manufacturing). In the process 1,200 employees were laid off. The Steve & John Show also ended in a Greek tragedy.

I survived the 1985 purge because I wasn't hitched to the Jobs wagon and because I managed (or had most of Apple convinced that I managed) the relationship between Apple and Macintosh developers. I was one of the middle managers who sculpted the reorganization, including selecting the employees who would be laid off and those who would stay.

We brought our org charts to a large conference room in DeAnza 2, the Apple building that housed most of the Apple executive staff, and wrote names on a white board. The people whose names weren't on the board at the end of two days of

button mouse, graphic user interface (pull-down menus, windows, desktop metaphor), bitmapped graphics, and integrated applications. In January, 1985, Lisa became a "Macintosh XL." XL stood for "Extra Large," "Extra Late," or "Extra Lisas" (in inventory). After the inventory was depleted and write-downs were avoided, it was discontinued in April, 1985.

1. Postscript is the technical term for a lucrative royalty stream from Apple to Adobe.

2. PageMaker is the Aldus product that launched desktop publishing. The creation of PageMaker was an act of God specifically intended to save Apple.

meetings were laid off. It was like being a master of ceremonies at a massive funeral, and I never want to go through an experience like that again.

The Glory Years

The Lemmings commercial was run backwards (wrong thing, right way) at the Apple sales conference in August, 1985 in San Diego, California. The tag line this time was, "1986 won't be like 1985." It was correct because the introduction of PageMaker in July, 1985 and the introduction of the Macintosh Plus in January, 1986 catalyzed the Ascension of Macintosh.

The creation of a new market called Desktop Publishing along with a faster, larger capacity Macintosh sparked an acceleration in Macintosh sales. Also, the amount of Macintosh software was doubling every year. After that, it was easy. How hard could it be when you had the best computer and the best collection of software?

Looking Back

Many people have written about the development and intro-duction of Macintosh by conducting interviews and background research.[1] Their books and articles focused on the intriguing and controversial problems—Steve and John, negative "Steve-isms," and the internal politics. I guess that stuff sells, but they miss the point. They try to tell you what happened, not what it means.

Typically, this is the story line:
Steve was bored at his own company. He needed something to do. He formed this exclusive club called the Macintosh Division. They (and he) pissed off everyone (and each other). Somehow they shipped a remarkable computer called Macintosh.

---

1. On page 279 of *West of Eden*, Frank Rose writes about a dinner party at Al Eisenstat's house (Apple's general counsel at the time). He describes Al's den as having "a view of the driveway and the tree-shaded streets of Atherton." Al's den at the time overlooked a deck which overlooked his pool which overlooked a grove of eucalyptus trees in his neighbor's backyard, and the driveway was on the other side of the house. Where do these guys come up with stuff like this? There is a difference between writing and typing.

It didn't sell very well. The Macintosh Division crumbled because Steve wasn't a manager, his troops were bickering, and customers were antagonized. The Macintosh Division couldn't revise and enhance Macintosh and developers couldn't deliver software and peripherals. For the good of the company John 86ed Steve. Steve started NeXT.[1] Things started to turn around for Apple.

This is what actually happened:
Steve, the Macintosh Division, and Apple blew a hole in the side of the invincible IBM ship. Along the way, we suffered through calamities, in-fighting, and strife. After the introduction, we were physically and emotionally exhausted. Bringing Macintosh to market was an impossible act to follow, and this, combined with our physical and emotional fragility, caused us to stumble and fall. Nevertheless, a core of true believers—Apple employees, developers, and early Macintosh owners—sustained Macintosh and made it successful.

This is what it means:
A small team of bright, fearless, and ambitious punks led by a charismatic high priest trying to do the right thing can defeat mediocrity and the status quo. The battle can cost a lot (even the life of the high priest), but it is so magnificent that the toll almost doesn't matter. Winning the battle doesn't require huge resources if people buy into your dream. Afterward, it's all worth it, and the revisionist historians say, "I knew that they would succeed."

Exercise

This one is for Macintosh aficionados only. I got the idea from a current Apple employee whose identity I shall keep confidential (thanks, JD).

The idea is that Apple should employ Andy Hertzfeld as

---

1. NeXT is the computer company that Steve started after he was purged from Apple. Almost everyone hopes he succeeds (some only secretly). A few Apple employees have gone to NeXT to relive their youth. Some of them returned to Apple because youth is overrated.

Keeper of The Way. All of the Apple engineers would have to explain their projects to Andy and then listen to his feedback. They wouldn't have to do what he said, just listen to him.

If you agree, send this mail-in card to Jean-Louis:

Jean-Louis Gassée
Apple Computer, Inc.
20525 Mariani Ave.
M/S 27I
Cupertino, CA 95014

Dear Jean-Louis,
I agree with Guy. I think that you should employ Andy Hertzfeld as Keeper of The Way.

_____

Name

_____

Company

_____

Address

_____

City   State   Zip

Doing the
Right Thing

Part 2

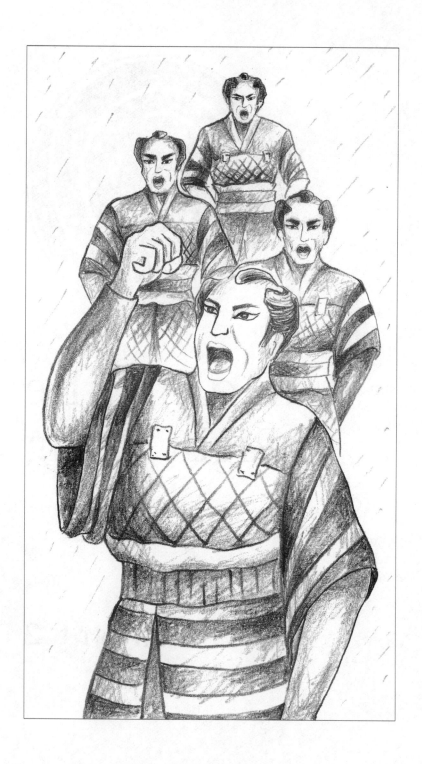

Environment

I don't want yes-men around me. I want everybody to tell me the truth even if it costs them their jobs.
Samuel Goldwyn

Perspective

This chapter is about creating the right environment in a high-technology company. It is the most important chapter of the book because people are the most important asset of a company. The right company environment is the first essential ingredient of the Macintosh Way.

The right environment is created by passion and sustains action, risk-taking, and fun. It is necessary because the high-tech marketplace changes so rapidly. For example, in 1984 Macintosh was a toy that was dismissed by IBM. Three years later it was a powerful workstation that IBM was trying to imitate. IBM is still trying, but without much luck.

In high technology you never have enough data to make a completely informed decision, there are few precedents to copy, and the landscape changes as you try to paint it. It's like shooting at a moving target from a moving platform in pitch-black darkness. Because of the rapid change, you need an organization that can quickly move, decide, change, and adapt.

The Top Guy

The starting point for the right environment is the guy[1] at the

---

1. The top guy doesn't have to be a man. For simplicity's sake and only for simplicity's sake, I use masculine pronouns throughout the book. If you don't

top. Every organization reflects the personality of the top guy, and if the top guy changes so does the organization: people who don't share his vision leave, those who stay act differently, and a different kind of person gets hired.

The founder is often still running a Macintosh Way company so there's no need to worry about finding the right top guy. Mike Boich (Radius), John Warnock (Adobe Systems), Paul Brainerd (Aldus), and Bill Gates (Microsoft) are founders who are still the top guys of their companies. This means that you don't always have to replace the founders with professional managers as the company gets larger.

In status quo companies, the founders have often left and the current top guy was recruited from a competitor. The logic was "he was there when they went through tremendous growth so he can do it for us, too." He probably had little to do with anything good that happened at the other company. Correlation seldom equals causation in high-technology businesses.

Let's assume, though perhaps we shouldn't, a baseline of intelligence, honesty, and diligence. Beyond that, being the top guy of a Macintosh Way company requires five special characteristics. If your top guy has all of these qualities, he can inspire your company to greatness.

1 ▶ Passion for products. Whether the top guy is a founder or not, he must have a passion for products. This kind of top guy creates a company that brings great products to market. Charlie Jackson of Silicon Beach Software told the Dark Castle[1] development team to create a game so great that "when competitors saw it, they would give up." It took a year and a half to finish Dark Castle, and over 60,000 copies have been sold.

When Bill Gates created the product specification for Excel, he told the programmers to write the "best spreadsheet possible for a personal computer." His kind of passion inspires great

---

like it, I'll send you the file and you can replace all the "hes" with "shes." Sexism is how you feel about the roles of men and women, not the use of pronouns.

1. Dark Castle is a game that has caused the loss of more productivity than any other Macintosh product to date.

achievements. Imagine working for a company whose chairman told you to create the best possible product and then was smart enough to know when you did it.

2 ▶ Strong sense of security. The right top guy hires people who are better than he is because it is impossible for anyone to be good at sales, marketing, engineering, finance, and operations. Steve Jobs was a good example of someone with a strong sense of security (what an understatement!) who wanted to hire only the best people. He used to rant and rave whenever a candidate was beneath his standards. He would scream, "A players hire A players. B players hire C players. You want to hire him? Are you brain damaged?"

Exercise

If A players hire A players and B players hire C players, how do B players get hired?

An insecure person would not have recruited John Sculley. Sculley was president of Pepsi at the time, and quite well known in American industry. He had his picture on the cover of Business Week at age 34. In retrospect, Steve was so secure that he hired a person who was strong enough to throw him out of his own company. He couldn't conceive of anyone taking his power. That's pretty secure.

3 ▶ Willingness to give employees rope. The right top guy focuses the company on the end results and gives his employees enough rope to accomplish great things. There is too much going on in a high-technology company to control everything, and giving people rope is the only way to make them grow.

My job at Apple was to "get Macintosh software." Steve and Mike Murray established the goal and got out of the way. They didn't tell me how to do it, nor did they care what I did so long as I delivered. It was their willingness to give me the rope that forced me to learn and grow.

31

4 ▶ Ability to live vicariously. Being secure enough to hire good employees and open enough to give them rope is a fine start. Being able to live vicariously through their accomplishments guarantees success. This means that the top guy should get as much satisfaction from his employees getting glory as he would from getting glory himself.

The ultimate top guy believes that the success of a company is because of his employees. The failure of a company is his fault alone. It's very hard to find an example of this because the people who start companies often have strong egos and cannot share the glory.

5 ▶ Chutzpah.[1] The final special characteristic is chutzpah. The perfect market has no established competitors, it's growing at 50 percent a year, and there are high barriers for entry for everyone except you. Wake up and smell the silicon. There are no such markets. A Macintosh company makes up for a lack of capital and brand-name awareness with chutzpah, and chutzpah starts at the top.

Steve is off the scale when it comes to chutzpah. He used a slide in the 1985 shareholders' meeting showing a mock-up of *The Wall Street Journal* with the headline, "Apple Proposes Detente with IBM." Most Apple employees admired Steve's chutzpah. Macintosh Division employees even believed him.

The great thing about chutzpah is that it inspires people to exceed their capabilities. Steve wanted to defeat IBM, not "achieve 18 percent market share." Epic battles are not measured in market share percentage points, and people will fight to the death if they are led by a top guy with chutzpah. That's why we worked 90 hours a week in the Macintosh Division.

Hiring the Right People
The next step to the right environment is finding and hiring the

---

1. Chutzpah is a Yiddish term for something daring that you did. It should not be confused with "unmitigated gall" which is a goyish term for something daring that your enemy did. A low-level example of chutzpah is someone who pirates software then calls the company to complain that there are bugs in it.

right people. These are the qualities to look for in the right employees:

1 ▸ Passion. Passion should be flowing through the arteries of every employee in a company, not only the top guy. Not everyone believes in passion—during the Silver Surfer affair Mike Stone of Ashton-Tate went into father-hoses-best mode and told me, "Guy, you shouldn't get so upset about Silver Surfer. Don't take it personally. Step back and look at the big picture. It's better for Macintosh that Apple give Silver Surfer to Ashton-Tate."

He didn't understand how passionate I felt about Macintosh, evangelism, and 4th Dimension. To me, the big picture was making Macintosh successful. To do that, Macintosh needed a high-end database. Ashton-Tate wasn't going to deliver one, so Alain and I found another way: acquiring 4th Dimension. People are not always passionate. That's okay—but don't hire them. Try not to let them upset you either.

2 ▸ High bandwidth.[1] A high bandwidth is necessary to understand a rapidly changing marketplace, make decisions, and keep

---

1. Bandwidth refers to the ability to assimilate data as it is about to make your head explode. It should not be confused with "bandwagon" which is something that everyone jumps on after the risks are over.

moving toward a goal. In a choice between high bandwidth and experience, high bandwidth is preferable because experience is frequently a false god. It's better to hire people who can get you to where you want to be than people who profess to have been there before.

Marylène made me president of ACIUS although I had never run a software company before and didn't know much about databases. (Let me burst a bubble: I never really used 4th Dimension before I resigned from Apple. I tried to twice. The first time I took it home on 800K disks, but the drive in my Macintosh at home could only read 400K disks. The second time I had it loaded on a hard disk that couldn't be connected to my Macintosh at home). Marylène believed that I had the bandwidth to understand how to start a company and sell a database.

3 ▶ Ability to deal with stress and ambiguity. Working in a high-growth company is stressful because of the pace of change. If the stress of fast growth, changing technology, and bitter competition weren't enough, there is also a great deal of ambiguity. There is only enough data to cause paralysis—never enough to make a perfect decision—so your employees must be able to deal with stress and ambiguity.

4 ▶ High energy. The tasks will be difficult, and the hours will be long, so sustained bursts of high energy are required in high technology. Steve made sweatshirts for the Macintosh Division that said "90 hours a week and loving it" to commemorate our work style. If Steve had built a sushi bar and installed a washer and dryer, we would have never left the building. All of the passion, bandwidth, and ability to deal with stress is for naught unless your employees have enough physical and mental energy to apply them.

Macintosh Values
The final step to the right environment is establishing the right company values. When Steve and Mike Murray told me to "get

software. We don't care how," I went charging off like a wild elephant, and in my fervor and zeal antagonized many people in the Apple II Division, Apple corporate, and field sales.

The atmosphere in the Macintosh Division was rather Californian and Machiavellian. Californian because we wanted to make the world better. Machiavellian because this end justified the means. These were the values of the Macintosh Division:

1 ▸ Ask forgiveness, not permission. When red tape and corporate policies get in the way, Macintosh Way employees do the right thing and ask for forgiveness later. As one example, Mike Boich and I created a mail-order business to sell prerelease copies of *Inside Macintosh* to Macintosh developers. It was not published in book form until 1985, so we had to sell photocopied versions to enable developers to write software.

At one point, we were selling 1,000 copies a month at $150 a copy despite an Apple policy not to sell anything via mail order. (This policy was put into place because Apple had filed a number of lawsuits against dealers who were selling Apple hardware by mail. Apple's legal contention was that Apple products require support and set-up and therefore shouldn't be sold through the mail. Selling *Inside Macintosh* through the mail would make Apple look hypocritical.)

As a second example, we loosened up the requirements to qualify for the Apple Certified Developer Program.[1] There were strict limitations on who could qualify as an Apple certified developer and how much equipment one could buy at 50 percent discounts for development purposes. Apple instituted these rules to protect the dealer channel. We loosened up the rules to cast as wide a net as possible, and developers bought more Macintoshes than the Apple national account and value added reseller channels for years. Many of the Macintoshes were

---

1. The Apple Certified Developer Program was implemented to encourage developers to create hardware and software products for Apple's computers. When a company became certified, it could buy equipment at a discount, receive informational mailings, attend conferences, and generally get their reality distorted by us.

bought for friends and relatives, but in 1984 and 1985 any Macintosh in the field helped sell more Macintoshes.

2 ▶ Placate the people you can't avoid and avoid the people you can't placate. In 1985 one of the reasons for the delay in Macintosh software was the difficulty programmers had obtaining technical documentation and tools. There were about five different channels inside and outside of Apple that sold these products, but each channel was poorly publicized and provided little or no customer contact. The process of "shrink-wrapping"[1] Apple's development tools also added 3–6 months of delays because of meaningless things like pretty packaging and bound documentation. In addition, Apple dealers were not interested in selling products that were low-volume and low-margin but required high support.

Dan Cochran and Lyn Termeer of Apple made it their goal to create an effective distribution channel for these kinds of products by placating some people and avoiding others. These are the problems they had to overcome:

First, Apple had recently gone through the layoffs of the Summer of 1985, and no Apple executive would seriously think of adding headcount to create an association for nerds. Dan and Lyn wanted to ensure that the association wouldn't be dismantled in the heat of earnings-per-share paranoia if Apple's sales dropped and 1985 happened again.

Secondly, they were proposing a mail-order business on a far larger scale than selling copies of *Inside Macintosh*. Apple's legal position that hardware required the face-to-face support of dealers would be weakened by selling technical products, development tools, and documentation.

Thirdly, many Apple sales and marketing people did not want to upset dealers. They were afraid dealers would conclude that Apple would start selling other things like application software and computers through the mail later.

---

1. Shrink-wrapping refers to the process of wrapping plastic around a software product, shrinking the plastic, and shipping it out. It's something like a bar mitzvah (a rite of passage for you goyim) for software.

Dan and Lyn created the Apple Programmer's and Developer's Association (APDA) to create a distribution channel for development tools and documentation. They found a user group called A.P.P.L.E. (Apple Puget Sound Program Library Exchange) that operated a software mail-order business in Renton, Washington and convinced A.P.P.L.E. to operate APDA. Apple incurred start-up costs of $200,000 and $50,000 worth of Apple equipment.

In the process of creating APDA, Dan and Lyn had to placate the people they couldn't avoid and avoid the people they couldn't placate. They convinced Jean-Louis and me that A.P.P.L.E. could start APDA for only $250,000 without adding significant headcount or costs to Apple.

They assured the Apple legal department that these products weren't for general consumption and were being offered to a select group of people with special needs that could not be served through traditional channels. (That's why people had to *join* APDA and sign an agreement that they were nerds, didn't need technical support, and wouldn't expect any.)

Finally, they avoided the people they couldn't placate. Simply put, they ignored Apple sales and marketing people until APDA was a done deal. APDA was formed in August, 1985, and 20,000 people joined APDA in the first year. APDA was immediately a $6 million a year business. Beyond these numbers, APDA also significantly accelerated the development of Macintosh software.[1]

3 ► Implement before anyone changes his mind (or catches you). As Dan and Lyn proved, sometimes the best path is to do what's right before anyone catches you. Often you don't need to ignore or avoid people—you have to take their instructions and implement like hell. For example, Mike Murray told me to change the perception that Macintosh didn't have software so I bought 1,500 copies of products like ThinkTank 128K, Helix,

---

1. In early 1989, Apple ended the contract with A.P.P.L.E. and began to operate APDA as a part of Apple in Cupertino. As of this writing, it's not clear if this was the right thing.

Filevision, OverVUE, Front Desk, and MegaForm to give them to Apple sales reps and dealers.

In the process, I almost got fired for exceeding my purchasing authority by a mere $747,500. (I had signature authority for $2,500, and the total cost of all the software exceeded $750,000.) Not even Steve had this level of signature authority. Only John Sculley could authorize this large a purchase. Susan Barnes, then the controller of the Macintosh Division, tried to fire me. Now she's at NeXT—I wonder what Ross Perot[1] would say. I wonder if $750,000 matters to Perot.

4 ▸ Do what's right for the customer. This is the easiest value to agree with and the hardest to follow because doing what's right for the customer is often scary. For example, software companies are tortured by decisions to send out bug[2] notices that could ruin the reputation of their product and decrease sales.

1. Ross Perot is the founder of Electronic Data Systems and a major investor in Steve Job's latest company, NeXT. Recently, he sold EDS to GM. For a while he worked for GM, then GM paid him about $750 million to go away and not compete with them. He went away, but some people think that he is still competing with them. Maybe he's been sticking around Steve too much.

2. A bug is an imperfection in your competitor's program. Imperfections in your program are called various things depending on who you are: ACIUS—anomaly, Claris—unexpected result, Microsoft—wrongful termination, Apple—undocumented feature.

This macho book-writing stuff aside, it scares me when I have to make a decision like this. Some companies never do it—they wait until the customer calls. The Macintosh Way is to do what's right for the customer and believe that everything else will fall into place. Most companies concentrate on the press and analysts, not the customer—that's watching the scoreboard instead of the rim. If you concentrate on the customer, the press and analysts will follow.

Exercise

The press and analysts think that MS-DOS compatibility is necessary for all computers, but your new computer is radically different from MS-DOS computers.

What should you do?

A. *Announce that an MS-DOS add-in card will be available real soon now.*

B. *Claim that the new computer can connect to IBM mainframes.*

C. *Form a strategic alliance[1] with DEC.*

D. *License your interface to Microsoft so that MS-DOS will look like your computer.*

E. *Build the best computer you can to fulfill what your customers need and evangelize like hell.*

F. *All of the above.*

---

1. A strategic alliance in high technology means getting someone to announce that they are going to do what you know you would lose money doing. Typically it is heralded as a brilliant move by the press and analysts until nothing comes of the alliance for two years.

Exercise

Rank the following choices in order from most desirable to least desirable. Explain why.

A. *The right answer.*

B. *The wrong answer.*

C. *No answer.*

---

5 ▶ Go with your gut. Just this once I'll give you the right answer. The correct ranking for the previous exercise is: the right answer, the wrong answer, no answer. In most cases, you won't have all the information you need, and the target is moving anyway. You must go with your gut. A wrong answer at least provides data and helps you make better decisions in the future. No answer provides nothing at all.

Software developers like Living Videotext, Solutions International, Silicon Beach Software, Spectrum Digital Systems, and Aldus went with their gut and undertook Macintosh development in 1983 and 1984. They believed that Macintosh would succeed, and they didn't wait until the data was collected. Indeed, the data for three years indicated that Macintosh wasn't selling well. The Macintosh Way is to weigh the risks, but not be afraid to take a shot.

6 ▶ Burn, don't bleed, to death. Doing the right thing and doing things right does not guarantee success or survival. In 1986, Dave Winer and Living Videotext almost burned to death trying to finish MORE.[1] He was nearly done with the product but was almost out of cash. MORE was a great product, and I admired Dave and the efforts of Living Videotext, so I bought 1,000 copies of MORE and paid $150,000 in advance. He

---

1. MORE is an outline processor for Macintosh. It started life as ThinkTank 128K, but was enhanced so much that Living Videotext decided to call it, and charge, MORE.

shipped it and became one of Apple's most vocal supporters. It was some of the best money I ever spent.

The Macintosh Way is to make your best effort, put everything on the line, and swing for the fence. Even when Macintosh Way companies fail, they do it with a sense of style and the knowledge that they gave it their best shot. In the end, it doesn't matter anyway because all men are cremated equal.[1]

From the Outside Looking In

This section is for people who want to work for the right company. Here are ways to get noticed and hired if you are on the outside of a Macintosh Way company looking in.

1 ▶ Love and understand their product. A Macintosh Way company wants to hire people who love their product because they make enthusiastic, happy, and long-lasting employees. Therefore, the starting point for a successful job search is to learn all you can about a company's product. If you love the product and can envision working 90 hours a week to make it successful, proceed. If not, stay put selling soap.

Here's a guerrilla job search tip for you. Separate yourself

---

1. This funny thought is attributed to someone named Goodman Ace. I don't know who he is either.

from the other applicants by sending in a sample of what you've done with a company's product. Adobe, Aldus, or Microsoft won't be able to resist interviewing anyone who knows how to use their product. It also shows initiative, an understanding of their product, and a desire to set yourself apart from the other applicants.

Exercise

A computer company with a computer that boasts a graphic user interface hired several marketing executives with consumer goods backgrounds. The theory was that computers were becoming more like soaps and less like technology, so brand management, packaging, and promotions were the key. They tried to sell computers like soap and failed.

Which statement best describes what this passage means?

A. The company used the wrong recruiters.

B. Computers are not soap.

C. Consumer goods companies are lousy training grounds for high-technology companies.

D. You've got to love a product to sell it.

E. All of the above.

---

2 ▶ Show that you want to change the world. Macintosh Way companies want to change the world, so they want to hire people who want to change the world. Working for a Macintosh Way company is a cause, not a job, so when you submit your résumé or interview, express a world-changing desire.

Of all the employees that I hired at Apple, Moira Cullen best personified the desire to change the world. When she interviewed for the K-12 educational software evangelist job, I was instantly convinced that she wanted to change the educational software world forever. Her interview with me lasted about ten minutes. I asked her two questions: "Can you deal with controversy? Do you want to change the world?" Today she is the manager of the evangelists who work with Apple's largest developers.

3 ► Skip the personnel department and have a current employee carry your torch. The most effective way to get noticed by a Macintosh Way company is to have a current employee carry the torch for you. This advice would be in the "goes without saying" category except that few people do it. Almost everyone sends in résumés or responds to classified ads and hopes that someone in personnel calls them.

Current employees have credibility with their company and can help your application rise above the noise level. (Apple gets about 10,000 unsolicited résumés a month.) I got my job at Apple because Mike Boich was my college buddy. The human resources person handling my recruitment actually asked Mike, "If he weren't your best friend, would you still hire him?" My résumé would have never attracted any attention if Mike hadn't been carrying the torch for me.

4 ► Perfect your cover letter and résumé. This is obvious too, but many people don't do it. Your résumé and cover letter are your marketing pieces. They are going to get about ten seconds of attention from a busy executive. In those ten seconds, they better sell you. This is how a Macintosh Way company interprets résumés and cover letters.

Description	Interpretation
Typed	Behind the times
Dot matrix	Doesn't care enough to use a laser printer
Multiple-page résumé	Trying to hide something

43

Spelling mistakes	Too lazy to use a spelling checker
Includes a picture	Ego problems

To "perfect" does not mean to go overboard. When ACIUS first started, we received a leather-bound folio that included a cover letter, a résumé, and an 8-by-10 color photo of the applicant. We didn't hire him.

Exercise

Match the type of résumé to the appropriate action:

LaserWriter	*Hire*
Dot matrix	*Discard*
Selectric	*Scan*
Hand written	*Read*
Linotronic	*Laugh*

---

5 ▶ Demonstrate passion and people skills. The most important things in an interview at a Macintosh Way company are passion for their products and the ability to work with other people.

A great strategy (or at least one that would work with me) is to demo the company's product in the interview. You'd probably get a job at Aldus if you gave them an incredible demo of Page-Maker. For that matter, you'd probably get a job with Aldus' competitors if you gave them an incredible demo of PageMaker.

The ability to work with other people is also crucial. Macintosh Way companies hate internal friction, so prepare for an examination of your people skills during a job interview. Do the next exercise because you'll probably be asked a question like it in an interview at a Macintosh Way company.

Exercise

In a job interview you are asked, "What would you do if you cannot get another person in the company to work with you?" What is the best answer?

A. Write a memo to your supervisor to elevate the issue.

B. Complain to the person's supervisor.

C. Install a virus on his hard disk.

D. Meet with the other person and work it out as peers.

---

6 ► Don't brag about having an MBA. If an MBA matters, the interviewer will see it on your résumé. If it doesn't, don't bring it up because Macintosh Way employees despise MBAs. MBAs use white-out on their monitors to correct mistakes. Where MBAs go to class reunions, engineers endow chairs. Honestly, I have an MBA, and I'm doing okay. This proves it's possible to correct even the worst mistakes.

7 ► Don't be proud; just get in. Don't make the mistake of setting your mind on a particular kind of job when you are interviewing. Get into the company anywhere you can. If you are as good as you think and the company is growing, other opportunities will open up soon enough, and you may get your dream position. The hard step is getting into the company, not switching jobs. So don't be proud; just get in.

When Jean-Louis started in the Macintosh Division in the summer of 1985, he lowered himself to director of marketing. (He was, after all, the king of Apple France.) A week later he was vice-president of product development. In 1989 he became president of Apple Products. Not bad for a French immigrant.

Once You're In

If you get a job at a Macintosh Way company, here's a tip to help you rise to the top. Do what your boss asks right away—no matter when he says he really wants it. Nothing shows that you are on top of things as much as doing what the boss asks first.

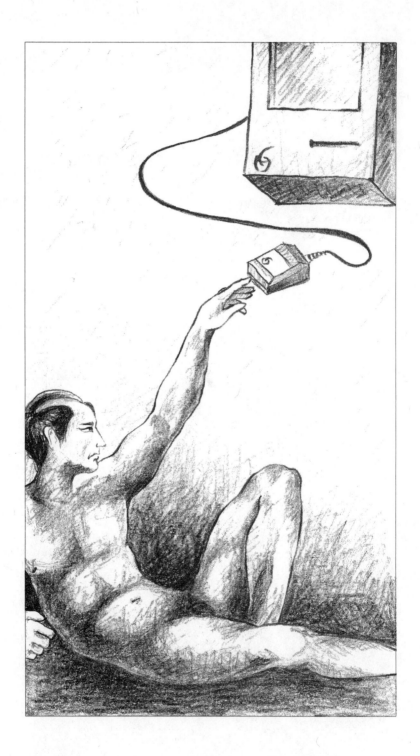

Great Products

Genius is an African who dreams up snow.
Vladimir Nabokov

The Foundation

During the layoffs, reorganizations, and turmoil at Apple in 1985, a core of employees, customers, and developers believed in Macintosh, and one thing remained the same—Macintosh was a great product. A great product is the second essential ingredient of the Macintosh Way. This chapter examines the qualities of great products, the right product development process, and the right development people.

The Macintosh Division realized the value of product superiority when competing with a giant like IBM. In the Macintosh Product Introduction Plan, the Macintosh Division clearly stated the importance of creating the right product:

...Yet when weighing the competitive strengths of Apple and IBM, we win in one key category: PRODUCT SUPERIORITY. It is our preemptive Lisa Technology at a recognizable price/performance advantage that will allow us to successfully compete with IBM for the next 18–24 months.

> **Macintosh Product**
> **introduction plan**
> **October 7, 1983**

"PRODUCT SUPERIORITY" is in all caps in the original—I did not add it here for emphasis. As Macintosh got better (permit me to include the selection of software as a part of a computer), sales increased, and Apple became successful. By 1988, Apple was selling about 800,000 Macintoshes per year.

Rolling the DICE

A great product is based on insight and inspiration, and it is an accomplishment—particularly in a world that tolerates and buys mediocrity. A great product is like pornography—you'll know it when you see it. There are four characteristics on which to base your judgement: a great product is deep, indulgent, complete, and elegant (DICE).

1 ▶ Deep—the product appeals to both passengers and sailors (as Jean-Louis would say). Great products are deep—they appeal to both passengers and sailors, and the passenger and sailor in all of us. A passenger gets on a ship, plays shuffleboard, and eats at the captain's table. A sailor weighs the anchor, goes into the engine room, and gets grease under his fingernails. Some people use a Macintosh to do what crayons do. Some people use a Macintosh to do what mainframes do. A deep product enables you to do both. Owning a deep product is like finding money in the pockets of your coat.

Canon EOS 35mm cameras are another example of a deep product. These cameras are auto exposure, auto focus, auto load, auto everything, but you can also manually control almost all aspects of a photograph. The passenger can take pictures of the kids. The sailor can use it as a professional tool. You can even hook it up to a personal computer. You don't need to spend $400 for a camera to take snapshots, but you will.

Exercise

Choose the set of words that best reflects the relationship between the two words in all capital letters.

PASSENGER : SAILOR

A. Policeman : Criminal

B. Chef : Waiter

C. Teacher : Student

D. Hacker : Nerd

E. Novice : Expert

---

2 ▶ Indulgent—feeling good (and guilty). Great products are indulgent. They make you feel delighted and a little guilty because they are overkill for the tasks at hand. A Mont Blanc fountain pen is overkill for signing books. A seventy-five cent ballpoint would do, but it doesn't make you feel good. Nor, frankly, does it work as well.

Macintosh is one of the most indulgent computers a person can buy. A fully configured Macintosh II costs about $10,000. A basic IBM PC clone can be had for $1,000. Many people think that a clone can do everything that a Macintosh can do and almost as well. It's not true, so people buy a Macintosh and feel good (and guilty). A NeXT computer is the most indulgent computer you can buy today, especially if you have a burning desire to model bouncing balls.

3 ▶ Complete—support, enhancements, and infrastructure.
Great products are complete. The concept of a complete product
is thoroughly discussed by William Davidow in his book, *The
Marketing of High Technology*, and I recommend that you read it.
According to Davidow products should include technical
support, a stream of enhancements and upgrades, and an infrastructure of power users, consultants, VARs,[1] and developers
that can help a customer achieve maximum satisfaction.

Great products are more completely defined than physical
parts like disks and manuals. Dave Wilson of Novato, California,
sells a stereo speaker called the WAMM (Wilson Audio Modular
Monitor) for about $80,000. When you buy a WAMM, Dave
comes to your house and installs it, aligns it, and voices it for
you. It doesn't matter if you live in "Bombay, India or the Bay
Area," according to the person who answers Wilson's phone.

Exercise

**Buy $80,000 of Apple equipment from your dealer. Does
he install it for you?**

Another example of a complete product is *The Macintosh
Bible,* edited by Arthur Naiman. It contains over 700 pages of
tips, tricks, and shortcuts for Macintosh owners. It covers material from basic Macintosh hardware to using specific applications. Since Macintosh information changes so quickly, owners
of the book are entitled to two free upgrades. That's a complete
book. *The Macintosh Bible* is probably the bestselling book there
is on the Macintosh, with more than 180,000 copies in print.

4 ▶ Elegant—ready and waiting. Great products are elegant.
They may have many features, but the features are tastefully and
transparently implemented. An elegant product will remind
you of Fred Astaire. He could sing, dance, act, and charm the
ladies with almost no discernible effort. And he looked great in

---

1. A "value-added reseller" is a rare (like the Loch Ness monster or Bigfoot) form
of reseller that adds value to a product.

a tuxedo. That's elegance.

It's very easy to find products that are not elegant. Microsoft Word is not elegant. It has an incredible number of features, but you almost need the manual by your side when you use it. Its features are one step beyond where you think they should be. People use Word for lack of a better word processor, not because they like it.

VCRs are not elegant. People never program their VCRs to record a week in advance, and the little 12:00 is blinking in millions of homes because no one can figure out how to set the clock. People only know how to play, rewind, and eject. There's a guy in California who charges $70 an hour to come to people's homes to set up their VCRs. He's particularly busy in April and October when daylight savings time changes. Someone could sell a lot of VCRs that don't have clocks.

The Macintosh IIcx is elegant. It weighs only 14 pounds. There are only two screws in the whole system. You can take it apart and put it together in a couple of minutes because the logic board, speaker, drive carrier, and power supply are all self-contained modules. It has rubber feet that you can place on the bottom or side of the case depending on how you like to position your Macintosh. There are even grooves in the case so you can slide it into brackets and hang it from the underside of a desk.

Acura Legend Coupes are elegant. They are $30,000 cars that successfully compete with $75,000 Mercedes and BMWs. They combine high tech (anti-lock braking, airbags, four valves per cylinder, and variable-assist power steering) with high touch (leather interior, clean lines, and four coats of paint). Mercedes and BMWs show how much you make. Acuras show how much you know. Allantés show how little you know. Porsches show how much you lied on the lease application.

Exercise
Call a Mercedes or BMW dealer. Ask him why his cars cost twice as much as an Acura.

The Process

The right way to get great products is a five-step process. The process is easy to explain but very difficult to implement. This is how it should work:

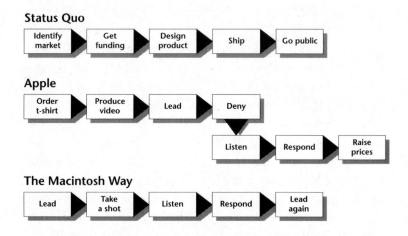

Status Quo

Identify market → Get funding → Design product → Ship → Go public

Apple

Order t-shirt → Produce video → Lead → Deny → Listen → Respond → Raise prices

The Macintosh Way

Lead → Take a shot → Listen → Respond → Lead again

1 ▸ Lead the market. The first step is to lead the market by satisfying needs, not wants. Macintosh wasn't what the customer *wanted* in 1984. Most people told Apple that it had to create an MS-DOS clone if it wanted to survive. The genius (or luck) of Macintosh was understanding that people *needed* an easy-to-use, what-you-see-is-what-you-get computer that integrated text and graphics.

The problem with listening to customers when creating new products is that they often have no vision or context. Ask a WordStar[1] user to review WordStar, and you'll get the gushiest review imaginable, saying that WordStar is the hottest thing since sushi replaced Cajun food. They don't have anything to compare it to.

Marketing-driven companies that go out and ask users what they want don't produce great, ground-breaking products. By contrast, in 1984 Macintosh gave people what they needed, not

---

1. WordStar is an IBM PC word processor. It is an incredibly deep product—so deep that most people drown trying to use it. But it has sold a lot of copies.

what they wanted. The status quo wasn't asking for these features in a personal computer:

Feature	Benefit
Graphic user interface	Ease of use and learning
One transportable box	Mobility
Bundled mouse	Consistent, mouse-based interface
Black on white monitor	Easy to read, simulates real life
AppleTalk built in	Inexpensive means to share peripherals and share information
3 1/2-inch Sony disk drives	Larger capacity floppy storage, protected media, and small size

2 ▶ Take a shot. You can anticipate the market, but you have to take a shot to verify your insight. This is the difference between Xerox and Apple. Xerox can innovate, but it cannot ship products. Take a shot as quickly as you can. Lisa was a shot, albeit unsuccessful, that verified a lot of the Macintosh vision. Truly, the Zen of the right development process is, "Ready, Fire, Aim." Do the product, then the research.

3 ▶ Listen. The third step is to listen closely. Macintosh, for all its brilliance, initially lacked features like mass storage, slots, color, networking, and communications. The market communicated these needs to Apple, and eventually Apple listened. After you've led the market, then you listen to it (a smart revolutionary listens to the people after the gunfire ends).

It takes a great deal of humility to understand that some of the best ideas don't come from within your four walls. At the 1988 National Apple User Group Conference in Ann Arbor, Michigan, for example, Bill Gates was seen writing down suggestions after he gave a demo of the beta version of Excel.

4 ▶ Respond. The fourth step is responding. Macintosh succeeded only after Apple responded to what it heard. The Macintosh II made up for nearly all of the shortcomings of the 128K Macintosh, and it clinched Macintosh's viability as an alternative to the IBM PC in business. This didn't happen very quickly, but it did happen.

5 ▶ Lead Again. The last step is the hardest. When a company achieves success it carries the baggage of backward compatibility and a customer base. It becomes unwilling or unable to break with old products, and blood-thirsty revolutionaries turn into blood-sucking evolutionaries. A Macintosh company has the courage to break with how a customer wants a current product enhanced and focuses on leading again.

The Artists

It's not hard to describe the characteristics of a great product. It's not hard to describe the process of making a great product. It is very hard to actually find the right people and do it. The most important factor may be luck. Some people went to college with Mike Boich. Some people worked at H-P with Mike Murray. Some people helped a French philosopher and historian.

Four types of people are required to understand people's needs and to develop great products. They are: Visionary, Architect, Producer, and Grunt. The Visionary anticipates the wants, needs, and dreams of the market. The Architect figures out how to build the product. The Producer keeps the team together and moving forward. The Grunt implements features. Sometimes all four people are combined in one—that's called genius.

Type	Function	Quality
Visionary	Anticipate market	Inspiration
Architect	Design structure	Organization
Producer	Catalyze team	Cooperation
Grunt	Implement features	Perspiration

Whether you are lucky or not, this is how to improve the probability of gathering the right Who of product development:

1 ▶ Respect the artist. Often a company considers product development to be an assembly-line process. In reality, it is an intellectual and artistic endeavor that very few people ever master. For example, 4th Dimension is the work of one genius—Laurent Ribardière. Products are intellectual and artistic accomplishments. They are not Lego toy houses to be rearranged by sales and marketing MBAs. If you are lucky enough to find people who understand what customers need and can create great products, encourage, protect, and respect them at all costs.

Exercise

If one programmer can finish a product in one year, then a six-programmer team can finish the product in:

A. Two months

B. Never

C. One year

D. Two years

E. Time for the board of directors meeting.

---

2 ▶ Create an environment that appreciates product development. Product development requires an environment that appreciates great products. By contrast, Modern Jazz is an example of MBA analysis suffocating a product. One of the primary reasons for killing Modern Jazz was its inability to run 1-2-3 macros.[1] This is like killing CD players because they won't

---

1. No footnote is necessary. If you know what 1-2-3 macros are, I don't have to explain them. If you don't know what 1-2-3 macros are, just buy a Macintosh and Excel or WingZ and don't worry about it.

play records. I heard that Lotus sold 60,000 copies of Jazz, the precursor to Modern Jazz, and got 80,000 back. Even the people who pirated it returned it.

A good environment creates an upward spiral. Where there is appreciation, there is great product. Where there is great product, there is appreciation. In technical terms this means, "Hire tweaks[1] who appreciate tweaks." Bill Gates is a tweak; therefore, he attracts tweaks. Microsoft is the only company that has been able to write system software, develop multiple applications like word processors, spreadsheets, and compilers, and master the MS-DOS, Macintosh, and UNIX operating systems. This didn't happen by accident.

3 ▶ Expose product development to the audience. The artists and engineers need direct and immediate feedback to improve their art. Most companies filter information and suffocate the team with a process like this:

The justification is usually, "We don't allow customers to talk to programmers in order to prevent leaks about features and delivery dates and to prevent them from getting ideas for new features." The problem with this process is that communication is slower, the nuances of customer feedback are lost, and your artists and engineers don't get the cheering or jeering emotional satisfaction of hearing it from the masses. Usually the process leads to products that satisfy wants, not needs.

In response to complaints about blinking 12:00s on VCRs, sales types would tell the engineers to remove the clock. Marketing types would add more instructions to the manual. (Most sales and marketing types take products that are born as princes and turn them into frogs.) Engineers would simply add

---

1. A tweak is someone who loves technology, often for the sake of technology. A tweak is never satisfied and always wants a better way. A tweak is never bluffed by hype. It's horrible being a tweak.

a lifetime battery and be done with it. Expose the team to the audience and let them hear the applause and boos.

Exercise

Solve the crossword puzzle.

Across
2. Designs.
4. The _____ of Us.
5. Perspires.
8. Opposite of Mercedes.
10. Quality sailors like.
11. Great products are _____.
12. All four in one.

Down
1. Catalyzes.
3. Anticipates.
6. Lead, take a shot, listen, _____, lead again.
7. Great products are _____.
9. Great products are _____.

Try it Yourself

Writing this book taught me more about product development than five years of working with Macintosh programmers and engineers. I fell into the classic traps of product development:

▶ I thought that I could write the whole book in two months and cover all the material in 100 pages. It took six months and more than 200 pages.

▶ I thought that I was "feature frozen" at least four times. Each time I added more features like exercises, footnotes, illustrations, and new chapters.

▶ I thought that the book was finished several times, and all I had to do was fix "minor bugs." Each time my beta sites pointed out major weaknesses and gaping holes.

I found that creating a product is much more satisfying than managing, marketing, or selling one. If you ever want to truly appreciate what it takes to create a great product, try doing it yourself.

One last thing: I thought that I had a publisher all sewn up early in the writing process. Then they backed out because they got cold feet. I learned how Laurent must have felt when Apple decided not to publish 4th Dimension. Luckily for me, Scott, Foresman immediately agreed to publish the book and they've treated me like an artist from day one.

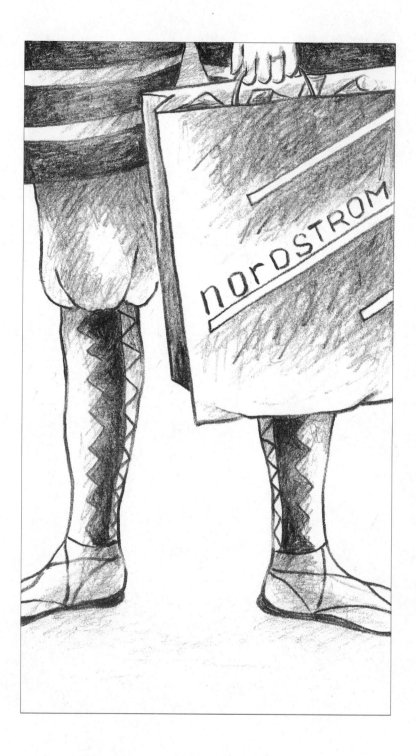

Support

*Remember that as a teenager you are
in the last stage of your life when you
will be happy to hear that the phone
is for you.*

Fran Lebowitz

The Nordstrom of Software

Have you ever shopped at Nordstrom? If you want to provide
great support, you should. Nordstrom is a $2-billion chain of
department stores from Seattle that is spreading across the
United States. You can immediately tell that Nordstrom is a
special place because they have a human playing a grand piano
in each store, not Muzak. They have incredible customer service.
A Nordstrom store forces improvements in customer service in
the entire mall. Great service—or support, or whatever you want
to call it—is the third essential ingredient of the Macintosh Way.

Exercise

**Call the downtown Seattle Nordstrom store and ask to
speak to Bruce, Jim, or John Nordstrom, or John McMillan.**

When Nordstrom messes up, it repairs with a vengeance.
Amanda Hixson, a former software evangelist at Apple, went to
Nordstrom in the Valley Fair Shopping Center in San Jose. She
waited for 40 minutes in the women's department and didn't
get help, so she went to the business office, borrowed a pair of
scissors, and cut up her Nordstrom credit card.

When she got home, her phone was ringing, and there were two messages on her answering machine. It was the manager of the store calling to apologize. As soon as she hung up, her doorbell rang. When she opened it, she saw a florist delivering the largest bouquet of flowers she had ever seen.

Exercise

If you rearrange the letters in "RDSOTMORN," you would have the name of a:

A. *Store*

B. *Philosophy*

C. *Family*

D. *Charge account*

The Way It Shouldn't Be (But Usually Is)

The Macintosh Way means providing support for the sake of doing the right thing. For a Macintosh Way company, support is an ingrained value that transcends the latest customer satisfaction survey and other superficialities. Because of years of dealing with the status quo, the customer doesn't necessarily expect good support or demand it, but he receives it nonetheless. Here is a topology of bad support from the bottom up so you know what not to do.

1 ▶ Apple. No support. No phone number. "Go back to the dealer." No upgrade path (buying a new computer is not an upgrade path). No alternatives. No one else dares to be this bad. Apple, not the customer, is in control.

I can't explain why a company that spends $2 million on a Christmas party and $2-1/2 million a year on t-shirts doesn't provide direct customer telephone support. Or hires only one summer student to fix ImageWriter drivers. Some things you simply accept, I guess.[1]

Exercise

Call Apple (408-996-1010) and ask for technical support.

---

2 ▶ The "Henny Youngman School of Support." This level of support gets its name from a joke that Henny Youngman, a stand-up comedian, has been telling for fifty years. It blames the customer for the problem:

I went to the doctor. I said, "Doctor, it hurts when I do this." The doctor said, "Don't do that."

The modern equivalent is:

I called the developer. I said, "Developer, it crashes[2] when I edit text." The developer said, "Don't edit text."

3 ▶ Bureaucratic Detachment. The customer, the support person, and the product are insulated from one another by a bureaucracy. Typical replies from the support person include, "It isn't scheduled for a maintenance upgrade this year" or "The product you received falls within spec." No one has control over anything, and problems are accepted as unresolvable facts of life.

4 ▶ Miss America. Poise, personality, and congeniality. A staff of polite, nontechnical people provide this level of support. They are taught canned answers to common questions but have no genuine expertise to offer. The customer still gets lost in the bureaucracy, but it is done politely.

---

1. Actually, I can explain the ImageWriter drivers—Apple fixes what it uses, and the last time Jean-Louis Gassée saw an ImageWriter was when he landed on Ellis Island. Apple did fix them, but I didn't notice because I don't use an Image-Writer either.

2. A crash is when your competitor's program dies. When your program dies, it is an "idiosyncrasy." Frequently, crashes are followed with a message like "ID 02." "ID" is an abbreviation for "idiosyncrasy" and the number that follows indicates how many more months of testing the product should have had.

For example, when United Airlines lost my luggage recently, the customer service rep politely told me that United would not reimburse me for any clothes that I bought in the first 24 hours after reporting the loss. I had absolutely no control over the situation. It was as if it were my fault that the luggage was lost.

The Way It Should Be (But Usually Isn't)

The problem with great support is that it is hard to measure its positive effects. By contrast, it is easy to measure how much great support would cost. Macintosh Way companies don't measure the cost or benefits of good support. They do things right for the sake of doing things right. Focus on the rim, and the scoreboard will be fine.

Here's how great support works:

1 ▶ Put the customer in control. The key to great support is putting the customer in control of the situation. When you shop at Nordstrom, you can go to any department in the store, gather items, and take them to any counter to pay for them. When you want something gift wrapped, they don't send you to a line behind the men's room. They wrap it, always cheerfully, at the sales counter. The customer is always in control of the situation at Nordstrom.

2 ▶ Take responsibility for your shortcomings. Great support takes responsibility for a product's or company's shortcomings; bad tech support ignores the customer or places a bureaucracy between the customer and the product. Great support provides workarounds or alternate methods to achieve the desired result. Problems are never the fault of the customer.

While getting a tuxedo fitted at Nordstrom, I lost two pendants that were Christmas gifts. We searched for an hour and could not find them. The manager assured me that their tailor was a long-time, trusted employee. After several weeks, the pendants still didn't turn up, so Nordstrom reimbursed me for the loss even though I didn't purchase them there.

I learned that Nordstrom takes responsibility for short-comings even when it's not their fault. By the way, several months later I found the pendants in the garment bag and returned the money to Nordstrom.

3 ▶ Don't point the finger. Living Videotext had a "no finger pointing" policy. For example, if MORE was not printing properly but it was not at fault, Living Videotext would call the printer, network, or utility software companies and get the answer for you. Companies that point fingers often leave the customer between two vendors who blame each other. The customer always loses when companies point the finger.

4 ▶ Underpromise and overdeliver. Scott Knaster, a Macintosh programming guru at Apple, has a son named Jess who loves Disneyland. Scott told me that Disneyland underpromises and overdelivers.

For example, if you get to Disneyland a little before it officially opens, they let you in instead of making you wait. Disneyland's policy is that children over three years old must pay for admission, but they never ask how old your small children are. When you are standing in line for rides, there are signs that tell you how much longer it will take you to get to the ride. But the times are purposely overestimated to make you feel like the wait wasn't that long. Disneyland says that there are no rain checks for bad weather, but if you ask, they give them to you.

Disneyland has policy and Disneyland has implementation. Implementation supercedes policy and delights the customer. Underpromise and overdeliver for great support.

Getting It

Fortunately, support is blocking and tackling. There's nothing fancy about it, and there are no short cuts. Nevertheless, support, like a Green Bay Packer sweep with Jerry Kramer and Fuzzy Thurston, wins ballgames. Here are five ways to great support:

1 ▸ Hire the right people. The right people for support embody three qualities. First, they are empathetic—they should bleed when a customer is not satisfied. This is the most important quality of a good support person.

Secondly, they get their jollies from helping people. Some people want to design products. Some people want to sell. Some people love to help people. That's who you want for support.

Thirdly, they already know and love your product. The most successful method for finding support people is your installed base of customers. If they express interest in working for your company, scoop them up immediately.

2 ▸ Empower employees to empower customers. The Macintosh Way is to empower employees to empower customers. The customer should control the situation, not the employee or the company. Most companies have rules against refunding money, sending out free samples, or accepting collect calls. The Macintosh Way is to do what's right for the customer, not adhere to rules, so let your employees make real-time[1] decisions to satisfy the customer.

Nordstrom's training program lasts one day: it teaches new employees how to use the cash register and then puts them out on the floor, fully empowered.

3 ▸ Integrate support into the mainstream. Support is not the butt end of a business. The services support departments provide are as much a part of products as disks and manuals. Unfortunately, many companies consider support a necessary evil staffed by grotesque nerds who were separated from their marketing twins at birth. Support should be a heralded and celebrated group—not overhead. It influences sales as much as your packaging, advertising, and PR.

---

1. Real time means people responding to events as they happen without having to wait for something or someone to give them control. It shouldn't be confused with "surreal time" which is the time between when a software company announces a product and ships it.

4 ► Provide the support staff with diversions. Support is hard work because customers seldom call to tell you how great things are going or that they understand how to use your product. Toys like radio-controlled cars, ping pong, video games, and foosball

tables help support people blow off steam. Jolt cola[1] helps too.

Good support people are also techno-junkies. They want the latest computers, stereos, video players, and automobiles. Companies should buy them as much as they can afford. It can even make good business sense. Customers often associate a company that has the latest tools and toys with leading-edge innovation.

5 ► Thank your customers. Try writing thank-you notes to a few customers every day. It doesn't take much effort, and the effect on your reputation can be amazing. The following message, posted on CompuServe[2] electronic mail, shows what one person thought of the practice.

---

1. Jolt cola is the purest form of sugar and caffeine. It is one of the few things that can accelerate the completion of Macintosh software.

2. CompuServe is an electronic bulletin board where people communicate with each other about meaningless topics all day and all night long. It is the closest thing to dating for a nerd.

#: 27443 S2/ACIUS
01-Oct-88 00:45:54
Sb: Thank-you notes?!
Fm: Jeff Segawa 76377,560
To: All

I bought 4D a couple of months ago, and as usual, I sent in the registration card. Normally, I assume that the things fall into some sort of corporate black hole.

About 1 or 2 weeks after I sent in THIS card, I got back what looked like a personally written thank-you note from Guy Kawasaki. Perhaps all Hawaii residents get something of the sort? I hope it wasn't because I was the only one who bought 4D that month!

Whatever the case may have been, one thing's for sure: I never did get any thank-you notes from Microsoft, or anyone else, for that matter. I'll just KNOW that I spent too much money on the product when I start getting Xmas cards too!

The Support Career Path

Dave Winer gave me a good tip about support. He thinks that support is one of the best entry-level jobs in a company. By definition, a good support person is a hard worker, a team player, empathizes with customers, and knows the product thoroughly. These are all qualities that promote success in other positions, so good support people can become great product managers, salespeople, and programmers.

Also, support people usually burn out after two years, and no one is a happier employee than a support person who gets liberated from the phones. So save your sheckles.[1] Don't pay headhunters to find yoyos from consumer goods companies. Look in your navel—the support department—for great employees.

---

1. Sheckles is the Yiddish word for gelt. You don't know what gelt is either? Gelt is money, but money is not guilt.

Support Success Story

You never know how great support will pay off. One night, Mitch Stein, the president of Spectrum Digital Systems, was working at 10:00 PM when the phone rang. He picked up the phone, and it was a vice-president of CitiBank who had a question about using Spectrum's product, TrueForm.

The vice-president didn't really expect to talk to a person and only wanted to leave a message. After getting the answer, he asked Mitch why he knew so much about the product. When he found that Mitch was the president, he was impressed. Citibank has bought more than 50 copies of TrueForm since then.

Late on another night, Mitch took a call from Adobe Systems. That call eventually led to the sale of Spectrum to Adobe.

Marketing

*The better the advertisement, the worse
the product.*

J. Gordon Holt

The Marketing of Technology

Marketing is the fourth essential ingredient of the Macintosh Way. Status quo marketing is the *technology of marketing*—expensive advertising and PR campaigns, 12-city rollouts, and come-to-Jesus videos; it is independent of product quality. ("Marketing" is not inherently a bad word. The status quo perverted it so that it now triggers thoughts of expensive and elaborate "campaigns" against customers.)

Macintosh Way marketing is the *marketing of technology*—finding the right people and getting the right information into their hands. The foundation for this approach is that customers have a deep understanding of what they want, how things should work, and what they are willing to tolerate. They are attracted, not intimidated, by innovation and technology. They actually use and like to use great products.

Exercise

A vector is a line that represents both direction and size. What is the result of adding the following two vectors?

Good Product (5) ➚➘ Bad Marketing (2)

Step One: The Right Focus

In football, defensive linemen slap the heads of opposing blockers to rush the quarterback. The principle is simple— where the head goes, the body must follow. It's a lot easier to move a head than a body. The tactic is so dangerous that it has been outlawed—but you have to get caught.

The Cult Theory

There is a small part of emerging markets called The Cult. It is the "head" of the market and contains hardcore power users and aficionados, plus a small percentage of luminaries, analysts, press, and dealers. The Cult is intrinsically elite, more discerning, less tolerant of mediocrity, and more willing to accept new ideas. It categorically rejects some products as forcefully as it accepts others.

If The Cult likes your product, the rest of the market and all of the layers are more likely to follow. Other luminaries, dealers, analysts, and press cannot deny what The Cult has accepted. Macintosh Way companies focus their marketing efforts on The Cult because it is the head of the market. If your product is great and your marketing message is true, The Cult will do a lot of the work for you.

Exercise

Send a StuffIt[1] document to anyone in the Macintosh community. The people who can read it are in The Cult. The people who can't are not.

The Pyramid Theory

In contrast to the Cult theory, some people think of a market as a pyramid of layers. The top of the Macintosh software industry pyramid, for example, is Apple. The next layer is developers, then luminaries, then analysts, then press, then dealers. The last layer is customers. The implication of a pyramid is that you can concentrate on the upper layers and work down. For example, you try to influence the luminaries, who influence the analysts, who influence the press, who influence the dealers. The dealers then recommend your product to the customers.

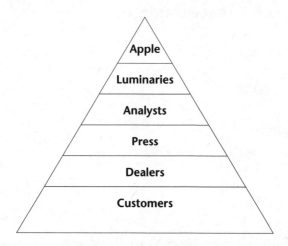

There are three problems with the pyramid theory. First, all of the luminaries, dealers, analysts, and press do not necessarily understand the customer or your product, so counting on them to transmit your message or to understand the market is stupid.

---

1. StuffIt is a Macintosh utility that compacts files to save disk space and reduce electronic mail transmission time. Everyone in the Macintosh Cult uses StuffIt.

Secondly, not all of the members of the upper layers have credibility with customers. *InfoWorld*, for example, is not part of the Macintosh Cult. *MacWEEK* is. Esther Dyson is not part of the Macintosh Cult. Stewart Alsop is. Expending marketing efforts on everyone in a layer often wastes efforts on people and organizations who don't matter.

Thirdly, most of the members of the upper layers are easy to influence, so their approval of your product can lull you into a catastrophic sense of security. All that really counts is satisfying your customers—not how much you impress the luminaries, analysts, and press.

Exercise

Choose the set of words that best reflects the relationship between the two words in all capital letters.

THE CULT : THE MARKETPLACE

A. Head : Body

B. Fleas : Dog

C. Flies : Cows

D. Wrist : Racquet

E. Editor : Writer

Step Two: Understand Your Product

The second step is to understand your product. An insightful and inspired product can open up markets, but you must understand how it satisfies your customers' desires to be successful. Apple positioned Macintosh as the computer for "The Rest of Us"—the people who wanted to learn to use a computer in less than an hour. Apple understood that it had created a device that could bring computing to people who had never used a computer before. It was more than a way to erode IBM's market share. It was a breakthrough.

Apple targeted "The Rest of Us" because it was not trying to steal market share from the existing market for Apple IIs or IBM PCs. Macintosh was going to bring computing to a group of people who never considered personal computers before. The "Rest of Us" positioning was so gratifying that people put themselves in Apple's crosshairs.

Exercise

Apple wanted to sell Macintoshes to people who had never used computers before. Which customer group would you expect Apple to concentrate on?

A. Fortune 1000 MIS[1] directors

B. IBM PC owners

C. Knowledge workers

D. Amazon indians

A ten-word description in the Macintosh Product Introduction Plan explained the details of Macintosh to The Cult. Apple clearly communicated its product, and The Cult communicated this message to the marketplace. This is the ten-word description of Macintosh:

Macintosh is an advanced personal productivity tool for knowledge workers.

▸ "Advanced" referred to Lisa technology. Lisa technology

---

1. MIS stands for Meshugas-Information System. It is the last bastion of anti-Macintosh sentiment in computing. Meshugas is the Yiddish word for crazy or nuts.

brought to Macintosh a user interface (pull-down menus, windows, desktop metaphor), bitmapped graphics, and integrated applications. The value of Lisa technology was reduced learning and training time, shared data across applications, and the enjoyment of using a computer.

► "Personal" meant that Macintosh was designed for personal use on a desk. A Macintosh was much lighter and smaller than an IBM PC, and it was going to improve information processing with a person, not the computer or MIS department, in control.

► "Productivity tool" meant increasing the productivity of a Macintosh owner. Macintosh was a tool to improve analysis, problem-solving, and communication with applications like word processors, spreadsheets, business graphics, database management, and project scheduling.

► "Knowledge workers" delineated the target market for Macintosh. Frankly, the phrase is marketing malarkey but it worked because it made people feel like part of a small, elite group. The phrase caused people to align themselves to Apple's marketing, and they persuaded themselves to buy Macintoshes. After all, who would want to be an "ignorance worker?" It is easier for the market to align itself than for you to do it.

Step Three: Get the Word Out

The third step of Macintosh Way marketing is communicating the right information to The Cult. Here are the key tactics. They are all close to the ground because that's what The Cult stands on.

1 ► Make sure that The Cult uses your product. The Cult is tightly knit and vocal, and it recommends what it uses. Make sure that The Cult—power users, developers, luminaries, dealers, press, and analysts—use your product by selling it to them near cost, exchanging for their products, or if you have to, giving it away.

Apple implemented a program in 1984 called "Own-a-Mac"

for the retail salespeople and sales managers of authorized Macintosh dealerships. According to the Macintosh PIP, the objectives of the Own-a-Mac program were to "get Macintosh into the hands of the people who would be selling it as quickly as possible and develop a knowledgeable sales force on Macintosh's features and applications."

Eligible participants could purchase a Macintosh for $750 (Macintosh started out at a price of $2,495 suggested retail). The Own-a-Mac program was a huge success no matter how you measured it—the number of Macintoshes sold through the program, the increased level of Macintosh familiarity on the sales floor, or moving excess inventory for Apple. I don't know of any other computer company with a program like this, but I don't know of any other computer that dealer personnel would want to buy with their own money.

2 ▶ Roll in the Trojan horses. The Ascension of Macintosh as a viable alternative to the IBM PC is proof of the power of Trojan horse marketing. From 1984 to 1986, the front door of most corporations was closed to Apple and Macintosh. The approved vendor lists of personal computers read like an IBM catalogue.

Macintosh entered these organizations in the Trojan horse called desktop publishing. The advertising, communications, and marketing departments bought Macintoshes for desktop publishing and graphics, not computing. Once the Macintoshes got in, however, they spread throughout other parts of the organization—even, God forbid, the MIS department.

The lesson is, "Don't be proud." Get in any way you can and let your product do the talking.

Exercise

An industry analyst asked the vice-president of marketing of a large, successful software company how he would introduce a product if he only had $500,000. The vice-president of marketing replied, "No company ever has only $500,000 to introduce a product, and I would never work for a company that didn't have more money anyway. Plus, we could always get more money from venture capitalists."

What does his answer demonstrate?

A. Venture capitalists are kind and generous people.

B. Industry analysts ask dumb questions.

C. $500,000 is insufficient to introduce a new product.

D. Large, successful companies often employ mediocre people.

---

3 ► **Kill the white space.** The Cult wants to make informed purchase decisions by gathering and reviewing in-depth product information. Therefore, your brochures, advertising, and point-of-purchase materials should contain an abundance of technical information, not white space and yuppie lifestyle depictions. The menu of The Brandywine Room, a restaurant in the Hotel Du Pont in Wilmington, Delaware, lists the caloric and cholesterol content of all its entrees. That's a tweak menu. The lack of

technical specifications, features, and benefits is a sure turn-off for The Cult.

Exercise

The Fullwrite Professional brochure produced by Ann Arbor Softworks in 1986 contained 1,000 square inches of surface area. Of the 1,000 square inches, 30 square inches were dedicated to product specifications and the rest to colorful pictures of Yuppies.

Calculate the ratio of 30 to 1,000.

---

4 ▶ Promote test driving. In 1988 Kellogg's put sample packages of a new cereal called Müeslix in boxes of Special K. Kellogg's enabled customers to try their new cereal before they purchased it. If you've got a great product, then a sample package of cereal, a loaner program like Test Drive a Macintosh, or a demo kit containing a limited version[1] of your product can significantly increase sales. If you've got a bad product, samples can be good for your competitors.

Loaners, demo kits, and sample packages also communicate a high regard for your customer's intelligence and purchase decision process. Don't throw content-free, four-color marketing materials, brainless HyperCard and VideoWorks slide shows, or Smurf cartoon characters at your customer. No one likes to do business with someone who thinks they are dumb.

Software demo kits containing a limited version of your product are good for one more thing: testing job applicants. The next time you get a job application from a redhot who professes to love your product, know your company, and understand your market, send him a demo kit and ask him to return an example of his work with your product. You'll probably never hear from him again. If you do, he's probably worth interviewing.

---

1. Programs can be limited in terms of the file size, printing, or saving capability. Some companies even sell limited versions as the full application to test the market for a year or two.

5 ► Give away blades to sell razors. The theory of giving away razors to sell blades is bogus. It may work for Gillette, but not for high-technology companies. Aldus created newsletter and business communications PageMaker templates—blades—to add value to PageMaker and differentiate its product from the competition's. Aldus makes money on PageMaker, not templates. Sell the $595 razor, and give away the blades. Better yet, sell both.

From Russia with Love

Denise Caruso, columnist extraordinaire for the *San Francisco Examiner*, wrote about the first issue of *PC World USSR*. Thirty pages of ad space were sold to American advertisers, but only four pages appeared.

The Soviet editors had pulled the other ads because they did not contain enough technical information or the information was already mentioned in the editorial. The Soviets have something there—advertising with content.

Exercise [1]

Parents who work in high technology often want to know whether their children will become programmers or marketeers. This exercise helps you predict the vocation of your children.

A child will become a programmer if any of the following is true:

Conception
A. *The baby was conceived while the latest beta version of a program was compiling.*

B. *The parents spent their honeymoon at a Macworld Expo.*

C. *The father made a t-shirt when the mother got pregnant.*

---

1. This exercise was inspired by Fran Lebowitz.

Prenatal

A. *Ultrasound revealed that the sex of the baby = 1.*

B. *The doctor heard the fetus humming Grateful Dead songs.*

C. *The mother craved more RAM, a faster processor, and Jolt cola.*

Childbirth

A. *The baby was born 18 months after it was announced.*

B. *Features of the baby like number of fingers and toes were not frozen at birth.*

C. *Immediately before delivery, the mother got pregnant again with version 2.0.*

Infancy

A. *The child refused to breast feed until the mother was checked for viruses.*

B. *The child's favorite Halloween costume was a trash can.*

C. *The child's favorite place to play was Xerox PARC.*

A child will become a marketeer if any of the following is true:

Conception

A. *The parents met at an MBA class reunion.*

B. *They bumped into each other the next day at a Ralph Lauren store.*

C. *The baby was conceived after an episode of **thirty**something.*

Prenatal

A. *The doctor heard the fetus humming Windham Hill songs.*

B. *The mother craved sushi, pasta, and decaf capuccino.*

C. *The mother got morning sickness only on the days she didn't have an aerobics class.*

Childbirth

A. *The father made a home video of the delivery.*

B. *The water broke before the contractions.*

C. *When the water broke, it was carbonated and contained no salt.*

Infancy

A. *Visits to grandparents were called "offsites."*

B. *The baby arranged his alphabet blocks into the word "MBA."*

C. *The first words out of the baby's mouth were "strategic alliance."*

D. *The mother reorganized the bassinet every two days.*

E. *The couple's second child was called Baby Plus.*

Doing Things Right

Part 3

User Groups

Whatever does not destroy me makes
me stronger.

Nietzsche

User Group Buddies

This chapter explains the right way to garner positive word-of-mouth advertising by working with organizations where The Cult and key influencers congregate. In high-technolgy markets, these organizations are called user groups. They contain the kind of people whom everyone else asks, "What do you own? What should I buy?"

For example, Jim Young, assistant to the president of Electronic Data Systems[1] is one of the original members of the Apple Corps of Dallas user group. You probably can't get an appointment with him, but he may be at your user group demo.

A good way to think of user groups is as a *medium*—like print or television. The difference is that a company cannot buy advertising in the user group media; it has to earn it. User groups and organizations like them are critical to getting the right word-of-mouth advertising and reputation for any company.

The Berkeley Macintosh Users Group (BMUG—pronounced bee-mug) is the quintessential example of the Macintosh user group phenomenon: it has an office, full-time staff, volunteer help lines, and a huge public domain software library. BMUG's mission statement is "…to give away information." It's so on top of things that it quoted from this book six months before it

---

1. This is the same Electronic Data Systems that Ross Perot started. Ross is the guy who hangs around Steve too much.

was printed (from *About BMUG,* January 1989. Reprinted without BMUG's permission):

Guy Kawasaki, president of ACIUS, and author of The Macintosh Way *believes, "BMUG is the quintessential example of the Macintosh user group phenomenon."*

The primary purpose of user groups is to give away information. There are over 750 Macintosh user groups[1] in the United States, and they have a total membership of over 200,000 people. This user group network helped sustain Macintosh when Apple couldn't. Members put in an incredible amount of time and effort conducting classes, publishing newsletters, and holding mini trade shows, with no reward other than the personal satisfaction of helping others.

Exercise

Apple has not provided user support to its customers. Thus, user groups have formed to support owners of Apple equipment. This development can be best described as:

A. Manifest Destiny

B. Industrial Revolution

C. Emancipation Proclamation

D. Cold War

E. Divine Intervention

F. Red Scare

---

1. If you'd like to find the Apple user group nearest you, call Apple's referral number. It's 800-538-9696, extension 500. If you'd like to start a user group, contact the User Group Connection at Apple in Cupertino for a copy of their handbook called *Just Add Water.*

In addition to giving away information, user groups fill the social needs of people with a common interest to band together. BMUG, for example, bands together once a week on the campus of U.C. Berkeley.

What They Can Do

User groups can accelerate the success of a product or kill it at the gate. Effectively working with user groups can negate a competitor's larger sales force and greater resources because user groups will spread the word for you. Most people in user groups will never buy your product, but they will talk about your demo, spread your reputation, and praise your support. Their mouths are more powerful than any advertising.

Think about it. What did you do the last time you bought an unfamiliar product? You asked around, right? There's a truism in book publishing that word of mouth is what makes bestsellers (so tell your friends about this book); the same is true with software and other high-technology markets.

User groups can help you in numerous ways. Four of the most important are:

▷ Disseminating information about your product.
▷ Delivering large, enthusiastic crowds at no expense.
▷ Reducing technical support costs by conducting training classes and creating special-interest groups. (The Porsche Club of America teaches members how to maintain their cars.)
▷ Evangelizing your product in the companies they work for, even if the user group members don't buy the product themselves.

When user groups help you, they are assuming some responsibility for your success. They become virtual stockholders in your company and evangelize your company and product for you. The more people help you, the less likely you'll really need help in the future, and the easier your sales job will be.

Getting to the Heart of User Groups

Worming your way to the heart of a user group is simple because their members are predisposed to cooperate with you. Remember—user groups exist to give away information and huddle together for warmth. These are the four most important rules for working with user groups:

1 ▸ Make a long-term commitment. Working with user groups is a process, not an event. Don't show up only when you're introducing a new product. Send them things all the time. Visit them often. The goal is to become a regular guest at user groups, not a visitor. Mediagenic, a software company in Menlo Park, California, has an employee who is a full-time user group ambassador. His sole function is to visit and please user groups.

2 ▸ Send the president and engineers. Mediocre companies don't work with user groups. Average companies send a product manager. Good companies send the president. Great companies send the engineers. Incredible companies have a president who is an engineer. Daniel Cheifetz of Odesta, the developer of a Macintosh database called Double Helix, has created a cult for his product by demoing it himself. He gives the second best demo of a Macintosh database by a company president.

Charlie Jackson of Silicon Beach Software is another great example of a president who makes user group presentations. He once got a standing ovation from 300 people for a prerelease demo of SuperPaint at a NYMUG (New York MacUser's Group) meeting. Afterward, he stood around with a pad taking notes on what features everyone wanted.

Exercise

Count the number of times that your company's president has visited a user group.

---

3 ▶ Send them information and samples. User groups are a medium, so send them information and samples regularly. Be warned, however, that they spread all the information they gather. Period. This includes both timely news and brutally honest information.

Software libraries are also one of the most popular Macintosh user group offerings. User groups sell disks as a service to their members and raise funds this way. Providing user groups with test-drive kits, technical notes, sample files, and examples is an easy way to expand your marketing efforts.

4 ▶ Sell products at a low cost (or donate a copy) to user groups. Aldus sells PageMaker to user groups for $100. As a result, most user groups use PageMaker to create their newsletters, and PageMaker is the desktop publishing program they most frequently recommend to their members. Altruism does have its rewards.

User Group Skills

If user groups are such great organizations, why are most companies, particularly the mediocre ones, so afraid of visiting them? It's not user groups' fault. Most companies think they are coming down from the mountain to visit the heathens. Do yourself a favor—either do things the right way or stay on the mountain.

1 ▶ Don't try to fool user groups. A user group can detect defecation before it passes through your orifice. There is no question that you will get lynched if you lie. If you think that you can fool a user group, attend a NYMUG or BMUG inquest, and you'll learn a lot about user group intolerance of lies and mediocrity.

Exercise

Three Apple employees from the New York office of Apple went to the September 1988 meeting of NYMUG to demonstrate the newly announced Apple scanner.

When the demonstrator booted HyperScan, the audience was greeted with a message that HyperScan was not compatible with the version of HyperCard he was using. Luckily, a NYMUG member had the correct version of HyperCard. During the demo, it was obvious that the Apple rep wasn't familiar with HyperScan.

The Apple rep showed that he didn't care enough about his audience to practice his demo and presentation. He hadn't even booted HyperScan from his hard disk prior to the meeting.

The best title for this passage is:

A. *Many People Buy Macintoshes Despite Apple*

B. *A Funny Thing Happened on the Way to NYMUG*

C. *Compatibility Problems Sustain Macintosh Sails*

D. *How to Boot HyperScan*

---

2 ▶ Never wear a tie. Wearing a tie prevents closeness to a user group. The user group perspective on ties is, "When you ask a

Tie[1] a technical question, he has to find a T-shirt[2] to get the answer." (A note to company presidents who are not engineers: take a T-shirt when you visit a user group.) I have never seen anyone wearing a tie do a good user group demo. Charlie Jackson of Silicon Beach Software probably doesn't even own a solid-colored shirt, much less a tie.

3 ▶ Get straight to the demo. When you do a user group demo, cut out the marketing crap and get straight to the product. This story illustrates why:

Claris sent a local sales representative and the product manager of MacDraw II to the San Diego Macintosh User Group. The rep spent about an hour talking about the goals and strategies of Claris. He even showed a company video before the demo. It was awful.

Marein Cremer, the MacDraw II product manager, almost saved the day with her splendid (but short because the rep used up so much time) demo of the product. The damage didn't stop there. At the 1988 National Apple User Group Conference in Ann Arbor, the president of the San Diego MUG used Claris as an illustration of how not to visit a user group. No amount of Regis McKenna PR, BBD&O advertising, or Macworld Expo parties can fix mistakes like that.

Exercise

Attend a user group demo. Keep track of how long the demonstrator talks before the demo begins.

---

4 ▶ Don't concentrate on only the big groups. Visit any user group that invites you. The only bad user group meeting is the one your competitor went to instead of you. Most Macintosh

---

1. A Tie is the kind of pompous jerk who thinks that he's got something on you because he has an MBA, drives a BMW, and uses a Cross pen. A Tie always has a tan that looks like shoe polish no matter what time of year it is.

2. A T-shirt is the kind of pompous jerk who doesn't think he has anything on you just because he dropped out of college, drives an Acura, and uses a Mont Blanc.

user group meetings routinely draw 100 people, and smaller groups are usually willing to meet jointly with other groups in the area to increase attendance for a special visit.

Exercise [1]

If you want to visit a Macintosh user group, answer these questions first.

1. MUG means

A. Face

B. To rob someone

C. Macintosh user group

2. Life is intolerable without a

A. Marketing person at my side

B. Louis Vuitton briefcase

C. Bottle of Perrier

D. Fast hard disk

3. My favorite thing to eat is

A. Quiche

B. Sushi

C. Blackened redfish

D. IBM PCs for breakfast

---

1. This exercise was also inspired by Fran Lebowitz.

4. **If I do a lousy demo, I expect to get**

A. *Cheered*

B. *Booed*

C. *Mugged*

5. **If I get to a user group meeting late, I will**

A. *Blame my Rolex*

B. *Slit my wrist*

C. *Call ahead on my cellular phone*

D. *Blame my imitation Rolex*

6. **My favorite view of customers is**

A. *Through crosshairs*

B. *Kissing my ring*

C. *Returning my product*

D. *Telling me how to improve my product*

Military Macs

The smallest and most interesting user group that I ever visited was the Pentagon Macintosh User Group. There was more brass in the audience than at Pier I Imports. The meeting was right before the announcement of the Macintosh II, and the audience wanted me to leak its specifications like any other user group.

I offered to seed anyone with a Macintosh II prototype in exchange for a ride in an F-16. It seemed like a fair trade because most people either pass out or throw up in an F-16, which is exactly what was happening to people using Macintosh II prototypes. The Army offered me a ride in a Huey helicopter, so I countered with a 128K Macintosh.

They took me into the MoLink (Moscow Link) room and showed me the teletypes that maintain communication between Moscow and Washington D.C. (There isn't a "red phone" like in the movies.) It's a scary thought, but IBM PCs are used as the terminals for MoLink.

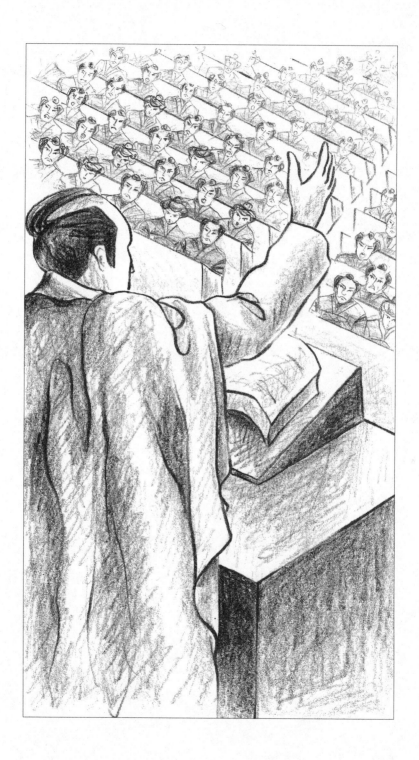

Evangelism

But when two people are at one in their inmost hearts, they shatter even the strength of iron or of bronze.
The I Ching

Seeing Your Logo

This chapter is about the right way to evangelize customers, user groups, The Cult, consultants, and developers. When you sell your product, people use it. When you evangelize people, they get infected, carry the torch for you, share your heartbeat, and defend you against your enemies. When you look in their eyes, you see your logo. A Macintosh Way company doesn't sell, it evangelizes.

Without the successful evangelism of third-party developers, Macintosh would have failed. When Macintosh first shipped, there was only MacPaint, MacWrite, Multiplan, and carrying cases. It didn't matter that there weren't any hard disks because there wasn't any software to put on them.

In 1984 we used to say that when burglars broke into an Apple office, they only stole the Apple IIs because they knew Macintosh didn't have software.

A solid base of believers makes it easier for products to succeed. For example, Adobe needs PostScript clip-art collections. ACIUS needs database consultants. HyperCard needs more developer support than all other programs combined. This is true for more than software and personal computers. In video cameras, for example, Sony tried to go it alone with the beta[1]

---

1. This "beta" has no relation to beta software.

VCR format and failed; now it is evangelizing other electronics companies to support the 8mm format for Handycams.

Exercise

Fill in the blanks.

In the beginning, Macintosh had only _____, _____, Multiplan, and carrying cases. After a couple of years, however, Apple's software _____ efforts produced lots of software. Now Macintoshes are _____ stealing.

Spreading Your Gospel

In 1983 and 1984, Mike Boich and I sold the Macintosh dream to hundreds of software companies by appealing to their emotions—making history with Apple, wanting to change the world, or helping Apple succeed against IBM. At the time, Macintosh was still months away from shipping, and the computer industry believed that only the IBM PC and clones could survive. Here are the basic tenets of Macintosh Way evangelism that we learned:

1 ▶ Sell your dream. The essence of evangelism is to passionately show people how you can make history together. Evangelism has little to do with cash flow, the bottom line, or co-marketing. It is the purest and most passionate form of sales because you are selling a dream, not a tangible object.

A typical meeting for Mike Boich and me with a developer would include the president of the company, the vice-president of marketing, and the vice-president of development. The dialog went like this:

President: "In order to undertake Macintosh development, we will require a development payment of $250,000 from Apple."

Vice-president of marketing: "We will require that Apple bundle a copy of our software with each CPU. If this is not possible, you must

feature our product in all of your advertising as well as buy one copy
for each dealer and field salesperson."

Vice-president of development: "We will require direct access to
your engineers like Andy Hertzfeld, Steve Capps, and Bruce Horn.
Furthermore, I want a tech support engineer assigned to our project
full time and available to write drivers for us."

Boich and I would rub our chins, ask them to wait until they
had seen a demo, and then blast into a performance with early
copies of MacPaint, MacWrite, Alice (a 3D chess game written by
Steve Capps), and Andy Hertzfeld's bouncing icon program.
After thirty minutes, either their jaws would drop to the floor,
their eyes would pop out, and they would have to wipe sweat off
their foreheads, or we'd go back to Cupertino.

If we stayed, we'd respond to their requests: "We are not
going to pay for your development. We cannot promise co-
marketing. You cannot call Andy, Steve, or Bruce. In fact, we
have only one technical support engineer for all developers.
And you'll have to make your program run in 128K."

Continuing, "That's the good news. Here's the bad. Our
documentation isn't completed, but we can sell you photocopied
drafts for $150. Also, you'll need to buy a Lisa for $7,000 because
a native Macintosh development system isn't available yet."

Then everyone from the company would respond, "When
can we get started?"

Exercise

Which of these evangelists is least like the other three?

A. Mike Boich

B. Alain Rossmann

C. Jim Bakker

D. Guy Kawasaki

2 ▶ Let a thousand flowers bloom. When you evangelize people, let a thousand flowers bloom. Don't close down opportunities for unknown people or small companies by concentrating on the obvious and established ones. When we first evangelized Macintosh, we selected companies like Lotus and Software Publishing Corporation. Theoretically, they had the resources, brand-name recognition, and talent to dominate the Macintosh market.

Luckily for Apple, we also worked with a thousand little seedlings in addition to the deadwood. The seedlings were companies like Solutions International, Aldus, Living Videotext, Blyth, Silicon Beach Software, Spectrum Digital Systems, Odesta, and Telos. These were the companies that delivered on the Macintosh dream and made Macintosh successful.

For example, one day in 1984 Paul Brainerd, the president of Aldus, showed up at Apple and demonstrated PageMaker to Bruce Blumberg, the product manager of the LaserWriter. The day before, no one at Apple had heard of desktop publishing or page composition. Aldus was a little seedling that grew into a big tree. At the time, most of us at Apple were looking to Lotus to save Macintosh.

We learned that working with only a few, obvious companies is like gardening in window boxes instead of fertile fields. Frankly, the established, MS-DOS companies had too much to lose if Macintosh became successful. As time passed, it became clear that this was an important lesson—let a thousand flowers bloom if you want some worth picking.

Exercise

When Mike Boich evangelized Mitch Kapor, at the time the president and chairman of Lotus, Mike wanted Lotus to port a personal finance program to the Macintosh. Mitch wanted to talk to him about "a new spreadsheet," but Boich figured that he had the spreadsheet category covered by Multiplan with Microsoft.

The best title of this passage is:

A. *Some Things are Doomed from the Start*

B. *Software Evangelism—Easy as 1-2-3*

C. *The Lotus Position*

D. *Why I Started a Hardware Company, by Mike Boich*

---

3 ▸ Plant seeds. In 1980 Joanna Hoffman was the fifth person hired for a special project that became the Macintosh Division. She bore the stigma of being the first "marketing" person in the group, and she was instrumental in the design, development, and marketing of Macintosh. One of her best ideas was the Apple University Consortium.

The AUC, as it was called, was a program to sell Macintoshes to the students and staff of a select group of high-profile and prestigious colleges and universities like Stanford, Carnegie-Mellon, and Drexel. Apple sold the Macintoshes directly to the schools, who resold them to students and staff at 50 percent off suggested retail.

At the time, the program was controversial because it bypassed dealers and many students were likely to resell their Macintoshes for a profit. The program, however, accomplished one very important goal—it planted the Macintosh seed in thousands of students as they entered the business world. As these students graduated, they evangelized thousands of businesses for Apple. They also provided a fertile recruiting ground for Apple's hiring efforts.

4 ▸ Never pay for anything. The software developers who demanded up-front payments and other *quid pro quo* inducements never delivered any meaningful Macintosh products. I paid a company to undertake Macintosh software development once, and the project failed miserably. The deal was a six-figure contract with Monogram to develop high-end Macintosh accounting applications. After Softsel sold Monogram, the new owners abandoned the project. I should have made 15,000 t–shirts instead.

The best allies work freely and enthusiastically with you because they believe in your dream. The worthless ones want to be paid for their efforts. If someone doesn't believe in your dream enough to take a risk, he will fail you anyway.

Ironically, the companies that demand money the most need it the least. This is true for three reasons. First, their management is composed of prosaic plodders whose goal is risk reduction, not innovation and leadership. Second, they are arrogant; they believe that the existence of their products gives a company credibility. Third, they are spoiled. They are so used to dealing with other mediocre companies that they cannot cope with a courageous one.

A good evangelist never pays for anything. If a company demands money, tell them what we told reluctant developers in 1984: "If you believe, you believe. If you don't, you don't." You'll save a lot of time and money. The people who believe in you will sink or swim with you.

5 ▶ Inspire, don't compete with your friends. In 1984, MacPaint and MacWrite inspired developers. The products showed them what a Macintosh could do and forced them to rethink their software. Unfortunately, MacPaint and MacWrite also competed with developers who were trying to create other graphics and word processing programs.

In 1987 MacPaint and MacWrite were unbundled[1] from Macintosh and sold as separate products to reduce this competition. Eventually Apple formed Claris to publish the Apple-labeled software and reduce competition with developers.

It's okay to show your friends the way. It's okay for your

---

1. Bundling software means including software applications for free when someone purchases a personal computer. Typically, bundling is done when the manufacturer doesn't think it can sell enough hardware so it has to increase the perceived value. Another reason is that the software might not sell on its own.

friends to show you the way. It's not okay for you to compete with them or bungle software. Make your money on the camera. Let your friends sell the processing and film.

Exercise

Choose whether these statements are true or false:

T or F   *Bundling software encourages innovation.*

T or F   *Calling bundled software "system software" pacifies developers.*

T or F   *Pacifying developers is not important after you have software.*

---

6 ▶ Pursue your friends after you've won them. Great evangelism is relentless—especially after you've won someone over. In many ways, it's like marriage: anybody can date and chase well; it's how you act after you're married that leads to true happiness. The bigger and more successful you become, the humbler and hungrier you need to be. I've shopped at Nordstrom for years and their service only gets better as they grow larger.

7 ▶ Exploit your natural enemies. Nothing crystalizes evangelism like a good enemy. Apple needs IBM. ACIUS needs Ashton-Tate. Claris needs Microsoft. A good enemy is so large, so powerful, and so established that no one expects you to survive the battle, much less win the war.

However, the lopsided nature of the contest between you and a good enemy means that you can define victory in your terms. For Apple, victory is making inroads in the business market. For ACIUS, victory is grabbing the lion's share of the Macintosh relational database market. For Claris, victory is throwing better Macworld Expo parties.

When Steve Bobker was the editor of *MacUser*, he told readers that the purpose of *MacUser* was to serve readers. He told management that the purpose of *MacUser* was to make money. He told his staff that the purpose of *MacUser* was to kill *Macworld*. Don't create an enemy, but if one naturally exists, use it to your advantage.

The Components of a Good Evangelism Program

If you are arrested as an evangelist, make sure that there is enough evidence to get convicted. The existence of an evangelism program is a sign that you want and appreciate your allies. This makes it one of your best recruitment tools.

Here are the key components of a good evangelism program:

1 ▸ An evangelist. A good evangelism program has a champion running it. This person lives and breathes the program. He is the figurehead, guiding light, and godfather for developers. He must thoroughly understand the company's product and technology.

Believe it or not, Nordstrom has evangelists, but they are called personal shoppers. They are the people who call you when special items come in, help you coordinate your wardrobe, and make you feel special.

2 ▸ Constant contact. Evangelizing developers is like bonding with a child. You need constant contact with them—talking to them on the phone, seeing their products, and taking them to lunch. A good practice is monthly mailings of technical notes, tips, tricks, and examples. Not only do the developers get information, they also get vibes that the company is on top of things and cares about them.

At ACIUS we push things a little far: we invite our customers and developers to come in and work in the technical support department. We get to know them, and they get to understand ACIUS. This is what one of our guests thought of his visit to ACIUS. His message was posted on CompuServe in response to a question about our developer conference that preceded the January, 1989 Macworld Expo:

#: 39361 S2/ACIUS
 26-Jan-89 00:02:10
Sb: #38813-DevCon info???!!!
Fm: Bill Hernandez 76656,3310
To: Paul Greenman 71211,3456 (X)

Paul,
We are under nondisclosure, however I can tell you this:

It was more than I ever expected by a (longshot)… I am still excited. It was worth the 6000+ mile round trip just for the one day at DEVCON. After Macworld I rented a car and drove down to Cupertino for a day in the life of Tech Support. It was really neat, to talk to the faces behind the phones, they all treated me FANTASTIC…

It was really nice to see the commitment to excellence very much alive at the new ACIUS facility, those guys work in a superb atmosphere.

All I can tell you, is make your reservations for next year NOW !!!!!!

Bill

3 ▸ Discounts on products. Developers are making a serious commitment of time and effort to a company and should be able to buy products at a deep discount. This lowers the barriers to adopting a product and shows them that the company thinks they are special. Apple, for example, sells computers to its certified developers for 50 percent off suggested retail. That's a bigger discount than dealers get.

4 ▸ Prerelease copies of products. A small, inner circle of developers needs prerelease prototypes of new products. This lets you get good feedback from power users of your product and makes your partners feel good.

The best request that I've ever seen to become a test site came from Rich Gay of Foresight Technology, Inc. It went like this:

As a 4D 2.0 beta tester, I would:
- *Dedicate 75% of my 4D programming time to "exercising" 4D 2.0, and documenting any anomalies, bugs, crashes, and other problems. I have three applications, in various stages of development, which I would use. Additionally, I would be available to test specific scenarios which ACIUS might be interested in.*
- *Testing documentation and reports would be provided per ACIUS requirements. At the least, I will provide weekly reports detailing my activity with the program, all anomalies, bugs, etc., and performance observations.*
- *Provide daily updates to ACIUS via CompuServe EasyPlex messages.*
- *Provide disks to ACIUS containing 4D files, procedures, or layouts when requested by ACIUS to aid in troubleshooting.*
- *Provide complete security to the office area containing the 2.0 program, and any written information or documentation. My office is protected by an alarm system which uses motion detectors and intrusion sensing devices to detect and announce unauthorized entry. The system is monitored 24 hours a day by Westec security. Additionally, only myself and my wife have*

access to my office area, which is my home. No chance of any
employees leaking or stealing anything.

As a 4D 2.0 beta tester, I would NOT:
- *Disclose, divulge, or in any way tell any person or organization*
  any information about 4D 2.0 or that I was involved in the beta
  testing program.
- *Allow the 4D 2.0 program, documentation, or information to*
  leave the Foresight Technology office.
- *Bitch about "missing" features or capabilities.*
- *Use all my time only working on my applications and neglecting*
  my testing responsibilities. I take the beta testing responsibility
  very seriously, and am willing to focus a large portion of my time,
  including evenings and weekends, toward that responsibility.

That's what you call a partner! If you ever want to be a beta
site for a company, send a letter like this.

Nice Try

By 1986, I was very proud of my evangelism efforts with third-
party developers for Apple. I believed that I managed one of
Apple's most important constituencies and deserved a big
promotion and a raise. I was so sure that I made this pitch:

Apple has 10,000 developers. If they each have five people
working on Apple products on average, this means that I
represent 50,000 people (about ten times more than the total
number of Apple employees back then). If they each spend
$100,000 on Apple-compatible product development on average,
this means that I represent $1 billion in research and develop-
ment (about eight times more than what Apple was spending
on R and D back then).

It didn't work. But as these statistics point out, evangelism
can truly increase the leverage of a Macintosh Way company.

To Market, To Market

The consumer is not a moron—she is your wife.

David Ogilvy

Through the Pipe

This chapter is about sales and distribution. It describes the right way to get products to customers. It follows the evangelism chapter because this should be the order of a company's priorities.

Distribution is usually a two-step process of selling products to distributors who in turn sell them to dealers. The status quo way of distribution is called Push. This means ramming large quantities of product on dealers and distributors because status quo companies believe that the distribution pipe will sell whatever gets pushed on it.

The Macintosh Way of getting product to customers is called Pull. Pull means creating demand so that customers pull the products that they want through the distribution pipe. Macintosh Way companies believe that the customer, not distribution muscle, is the key.

Distribution boils down to two simple rules: distributors stock what dealers sell, and dealers sell what customers buy. Inherently, this means that Push techniques will fail because customer demand determines what sells, not distribution muscle.

Distributors

Distributors fulfill two very important functions. First, they are shipping, billing, and collecting engines that service hundreds of individual dealers. It is much easier for a company to manage three distributors than 2,000 individual dealer accounts.

Secondly, distributors offer a convenient way for dealers to balance their stock because dealers can exchange inventory of products from different vendors. For example, if a dealer is over-stocked with Microsoft Word, he can return it to his distributor and get SuperPaint from Silicon Beach Software instead. This encourages dealers to purchase new products from small-er companies.

Distributors are usually the whipping boys of large status quo companies. In the personal computer business, compa-nies like Lotus and Ashton-Tate love to load up distributors with inventory. It's called a minimum annual purchase which al-lows a distributor to retain the privilege of selling their products.

It's easy to identify good distributors. The two most important questions you should ask yourself are, "Can they ship?" and "Will they pay?" In the Macintosh market, Bonsu, Micro D, and Softsel are very fine distributors that do both, thank you.

Dealers

Dealers, the second step of the distribution pipeline, constitute a more complex issue. They can provide a convenient place for customers to learn about products and then purchase them, or they can push customers out the door with products that are ill-suited to their needs. Unfortunately, the latter case prevails, but let's examine a dealer that represents the ideal.

About two miles down the road from the Stanford Nordstrom is a Macintosh software store called ComputerWare. It is a store that masquerades as a user group—it disseminates information and provides a social gathering place in addition to selling software. ComputerWare even sponsors a user group called MUCoW (you can guess how that's pronounced)—Macintosh Users of ComputerWare.

There is a huge difference between ComputerWare and most other computer stores. The staff at ComputerWare acts like volunteers who are there to help you. They don't pretend to know more than the customers who walk in—which could be one of the original Macintosh engineers like Andy Hertzfeld. In fact, they are among the best-informed salespeople in the Macintosh world. The staff of most computer stores act like they are superior to the customer, assuming he is ignorant, incompetent, and perhaps uneducable.

Exercise

Go to several computer stores and ask if you can test drive some Macintosh software. Match the store to the response you receive:

"What's a Macintosh?"	*Computer Error*
"Sorry, I only sell IBM PCs."	*Priority None*
"Don't touch the keyboard."	*Computer Minus*
"Let me open a package so you can try it."	*ComputerWare*

The Right Distribution

Like them or not, distributors and dealers are here to stay. They are indispensable to physically moving the goods from a company to its customers. They are not, however, responsible for creating customer demand. That's up to the company itself.

Unfortunately, many distributors and dealers try to erode a company's margin[1] along the way. The typical downward distribution spiral works like this:

1. Distributors and dealers want extra margin and promotional

---

1. Margin is the difference between what it costs to make something and what you sell it for. It's also the border around a page. It's also a way to borrow money from your stockbroker to buy more Apple stock than you can afford. A margin "call" is when your stockbroker calls you for more money because your Apple stock has dropped.

funds as an incentive to stock products and to "create market awareness."

2. Companies give in and sacrifice their margin to dealers and distributors. Then they don't have the money to create customer pull.

3. People don't go into stores asking for their products because the companies have not created customer pull.

4. Dealers don't sell the companies' products because people aren't asking for them.

5. Distributors don't stock the companies' products because dealers aren't asking for them.

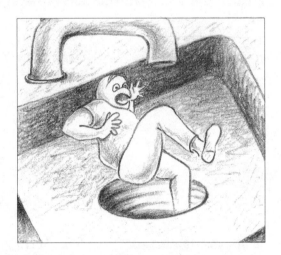

Good distribution means moving products through the pipe while preserving as much margin as possible. Here is the right way to achieve this kind of distribution:

1 ▸ Focus on pull, not push. Pull works. Push doesn't. If a company's product, support, and marketing are great, customers will demand its product from the distribution pipe. This whole book is about creating pull so that a company doesn't need to waste money on Push programs like spiffs,[1] dealer rebates, or

---

1. A spiff is one of the last legal means of paying people off. It usually works this way: if a retail salesperson sells a company's product, the company gives him a cash reward. It is a good idea when a salesperson really recommends a product

giving extra points of margin.[1] Test-drive kits and informative advertising are far more effective ways to generate sales than these Push gimmicks.

Also, stores like ComputerWare place a high value on their long-term relationship with customers. They won't sell a customer an inferior product for a quick buck[2] so the margin used up by Push programs is often wasted.

If you want to have pull, generate pull.

Exercise

Which of the following is least likely to create customer demand?

A. Great support.

B. Great products.

C. Great marketing.

D. Computer salesmen with new BMWs.

---

2 ▶ Blast it out. Companies usually try to control distribution. They try to create an exclusive group of dealers who sell and support their products. In exchange for the dedication of its dealers, the company protects them by not selling mail order, selling direct to national accounts, or authorizing VARs without storefronts.

I believe that you cannot have too many silk blouses, too fast a car, or too much distribution. "Controlled distribution" is an oxymoron. The right distribution is blasting out product and letting customers choose which distribution channel to patronize.

---

to ask him if he's getting a spiff to sell it. This may keep him honest.

1. "Extra Points of Margin" is the name of the Businessland company song. Compaq wouldn't sing it and deauthorized Businessland as a dealership.

2. What's the difference between car salesmen and most computer salesmen? Car salesmen know when they are lying.

Some customers will prefer the selection and social atmosphere of ComputerWare. Some will prefer the convenience of mail order from a company like MacConnection. Some will prefer the handholding of a developer or consultant.

To be fair, if image and status are important to a company's product, it should be more selective. Mont Blanc pens in airport newstands, for example, would be depressing. In general, though, a company shouldn't worry about protecting anyone along the distribution pipe. The organizations and channels that fill a need will survive.

3 ▸ Accept your responsibilities. No matter how great the dealer, a company is ultimately responsible for its customers' satisfaction. It is stupid to depend on even the best dealers to provide technical support for a company's product. Good dealers can sense when a company accepts its responsibilities and will sell more of its product because they believe in the company. If a dealer asks you for more margin because it is going to support the product, respond by saying, "Nice try. Can we talk about payment terms now?"

Exercise

A scorpion wanted a frog to carry him on his back across a river. The frog said to the scorpion, "How dumb do you think I am? As soon as we get to the other side, you'll sting me and kill me."

The scorpion replied, "Why would I sting you? Just get me to the other side, and I'll help you catch some bugs to eat."

What would you do if you were the frog?

A. Trust the scorpion.

B. Catch your own bugs.

> *C. Talk the scorpion into giving you a ride.*
>
> *D. Take the scorpion to the middle of the river and drown him.*

4 ► Forget the "Just Get" Solutions. One of the nasty tricks that the distribution pipe plays on companies is promoting the idea of "just get" solutions. "If I could *just get* Micro D to distribute my product." "If I could *just get* ComputerWare to put my product in the window." "If I could *just get* MacConnection to feature my product in their ads."

"Just get" solutions in the distribution pipe help some but they also defocus a company from doing the right thing and doing things right. Success is achieved through incremental changes that appear to happen at glacial speeds. Improvements to your product, marketing, and support work better than magical promotions for the distribution pipe.

Building the Sales Force

The Environment chapter discussed the most important qualities of employees at a Macintosh Way company. They are passion, high bandwidth, ability to deal with stress and ambiguity, and high energy. These qualities are necessary for a sales force because it represents the company to so many outsiders—customers, dealers, and distributors. Here's how to find and install a good sales force:

1 ► Recruit retail sales reps. One of the best recruiting grounds is retail stores for three reasons. First, retail sales reps are underpaid so they really appreciate a new opportunity. Secondly, retail reps understand what it's like to sell to users and, more importantly, what it's like to be rejected by customers. Finally, after dealing with many other vendor reps, they know how to do their job well. One of the best sales reps that ACIUS ever hired was stolen from Egghead.

117

2 ▸ Be wary of experience. Previous experience obtained as an employee for a competitor is not usually a desirable quality. It is better to work with raw, enthusiastic potential than an old pro from a competitor who will merely transfer his old habits to a new product and company. A company may gain some expertise, but it comes with a great deal of baggage. Also, hiring anyone from a competitor will mean that confidential information will make its way back to the competitor through old friendships.

For those of you in the Macintosh business, one of the worst places to hire sales people is from Apple because Apple perverts its employees. To an Apple employee, tough times means riding a 20-foot limousine instead of a 25-foot one. Horrible times means sharing a limousine. When we started ACIUS, I tried to hire a 23 year-old Apple intern for an entry-level marketing position. Our negotiations broke down when he asked for four percent of ACIUS.

3 ▸ Throw them to the wolves. The clock starts ticking from the moment the candidate accepts a job offer. A good rep will immediately begin to learn about his new products—even as he's serving the last two weeks at his old job. (This is also a good way to see if you've hired the right person.) If it's a Macintosh software product, he should start learning how to demo it so that he can hit the ground running.

Once he is on the payroll, give him about a week to familiarize himself with the company and product. Then send him directly into the field. In high technology, the market is moving too fast to go through a one-year training program. Also, it's good to find out as soon as possible if you've hired the right person, and there's nothing like a field trial as the acid test.

4 ▸ Reward the result you desire. Creating an effective commission plan for a sales force is very difficult. Some plans require a Cray[1]—percent against quota, number of sales calls, percent of

---

1. A Cray is a supercomputer. It costs about $15 million. It comes bundled with engineers, it's available in about 250 colors, and it can eat a Macintosh for

gross margin, quantity of incremental business, etc.

Companies usually have regional salespeople who are compensated for the sales they generate in their territories. Unfortunately, it is difficult to track products purchased from distributors, distributed by the central purchasing of national chains, and sold by mail-order companies.

Problems often occur when a sales rep successfully evangelizes a customer on his product and then the customer buys it from a mail-order company. Unfortunately, this does not reward the sales rep for the result desired—sales into a customer's hands— if the mail-order company is outside of his territory.

A plan that bases commissions on the number of warranty cards returned from each region avoids this problem. One way to operate the plan is to take all of the warranty cards for a month, calculate the percentage that each sales territory generates, and then apply this percentage to the previous month's total company sales to calculate commissions.

This plan works well for three reasons. First, it rewards the results desired: actual sales into customers' hands. Loading up a dealer's shelf doesn't count.

Secondly, it's very simple. The company only has to count warranty cards and doesn't have to depend on reports from numerous distributors, national chains, and mail-order companies.

Thirdly, it encourages the sales force to work together on customers with offices in many locations, because all that counts is where the card comes from, not where the decision was made or where the software was purchased.

An added benefit is that the sales force really pushes its customers to return their warranty cards. This lets a company keep in contact with more customers, send them upgrades, and sell them new products and add-ons.

---

breakfast. Apple bought a Cray to design the next Macintosh. Cray bought Macintoshes to design the next Cray.

Exercise

Match the type of commission plan to the results.

Commission Plan	Results
Sales into a territory	*Overstocked dealers*
Number of new accounts	*New accounts*
Quantity of sales calls	*Increased mileage expenses*
Percentage of warranty cards	*Customers buying products*

How to Find Good Stores

This chapter has concentrated on setting up a good distribution channel if you work for a company. Now let's discuss how to find good stores when you are the customer.

1 ▸ Ask a user group or current customers. Here's where that potent force called word-of-mouth advertising rears its pretty head again. The best way to find a good store is to ask someone who's already looked and been hooked. User groups and current customers are the best way to find a good store.

Exercise

Call BMUG (415-549-BMUG) and ask them to recommend a good Macintosh software store.

---

2 ▸ Shop where tweaks shop. You can tell a good Japanese restaurant if lots of Japanese people eat there. You can tell a good French restaurant if lots of French people eat there. You can tell a good Chinese restaurant if lots of Jewish people eat there. It's the same concept in high technology. Tweaks shop at a store for good reasons. Laurent Ribardière, Andy Hertzfeld, and Bill Atkinson all shop at ComputerWare.

3 ▶ Look for a store with a large selection of products. A store with a large selection of products can offer you better advice. Its staff is more likely to be familiar with more products and able to recommend the right product for your needs. A large selection is also a good indication that the store is doing well and is in good credit standing with its vendors.

You can tell a good Macintosh computer store from a mediocre one by the amount of Adobe fonts that it stocks. The good ones haves lots of Adobe fonts. The more it stocks, the better the store. Every store stocks Word, Excel, and PageMaker. Check out the Adobe font selection.

4 ▶ Find a store that schedules vendor demos. A store that has many vendors demonstrating their products is at the leading edge of products. Bringing in vendors also indicates a high regard for a customer's ability to make intelligent purchase decisions. Finally, the willingness of vendors to support a store shows that the store is important. Few vendors are going to waste time at a deadbeat store.

Exercise

This is a field trip. Visit ComputerWare to see how customers should be treated. It's at the corner of El Camino (the Champs-Elysées of Silicon Valley)[1] and California Avenue. If you get there early, Joanie's across the street makes great breakfasts, and Cho's, two blocks down towards the railroad, has the best char siu bao and pot stickers in Palo Alto.

---

1. Do you know the difference between Silicon Valley and yogurt? Yogurt has culture.

The Printed Word

Critics are like eunuchs in a harem:
they know how it's done, they've seen it
done every day, but they're unable to do
it themselves.

Brendan Behan

Advertising and PR

There's a big difference between advertising and PR. Advertising is when you tell people how great you are. PR is when someone else says how great you are. PR is better. (This is Jean-Louis' insight, although he uses sexual prowess when he explains it.) This chapter is about getting the right information to the right people by using an intermediary called the press.

Not the First Step

The first step isn't finding a PR agency, because hiring an agency leads to abdication of clear thinking. Most companies treat PR like disk duplication: "Let's not bother with it right now. Let's farm it out to a third-party vendor." The problem is that the third-party vendor assigns you a BA fresh from USC who is the nephew of the founder.

Most PR agencies don't understand a thing about technology. They have their cookie-cutter ways of handling all accounts: do an audit—report on the results—provide recommendations—get paid—tell the client to refer all press calls and inquiries to the agency—cut and paste press releases.

Don't get me wrong: an agency can provide valuable services like providing a sanity check on your marketing and controlling your ego (a full-time job for our agency when we had one). If you are doing things right and you have a good PR agency, it can be awesome, but you cannot substitute an agency and PR fluff for clear thinking.

Exercise

Go to a speech by a company president. Does he have a PR flack[1] babysitting him? If he does, ask him why.

Properly used, a PR agency can amplify good reality and play the heavy when you need to "correct" the press. The right PR, however, is primarily the result of four factors that you control: good reality, clear positioning, personal relationships, and PR smarts.

Good Reality

The first factor is good reality—the right company environment, great products, legendary support, and informative marketing. You can have the worst PR agency in the world (or no PR agency at all), and you will get good press if you have good reality.

Think about all the bad press you've seen. Wasn't it about bad reality? Bugs. Premature releases. Delayed shipments. Poor support. Generally acting like the south end of a northbound horse.

Bad press isn't a chicken-and-egg thing. Bad press reflects the reality of your company, not your PR efforts. The Japanese have a saying, "Wasabi[2] cannot fix rotten fish." Do right by your customer and you won't have to worry about bad press. Enzo

---

1. A PR flack is someone that you pay your PR agency $125 an hour for to tell you that you are great and to prevent you from making an ass of yourself in public. PR flacks, however, usually know less about technology than you know about PR.

2. Wasabi is a killer form of horseradish that is mixed with soy sauce to form a dip for eating sushi and sashimi. Macintosh owners eat it to show how tough they are.

Toresi, one of the founders of Businessland, told me, "There is only one judge. That's the customer."

Clear Positioning

The second factor of the right PR (and really all marketing) is clearly understanding and positioning your product. The best positioning statement is two to three words and defines the whole market—for example, "desktop publishing" meant PageMaker. The second best positioning statement is a short sentence.

Long, all-encompassing positioning statements like "a powerful, easy-to-use, multiuser, graphic database with procedural language and runtime capability" create confusion. A better positioning statement is "the most powerful database for a personal computer."

If you can't come up with a one-sentence positioning statement, something is wrong with your product or your marketing. Lotus executives needed a CD-ROM to explain the positioning of Modern Jazz.

Sometimes there is a bigger problem: the product was designed by marketing. Then there is no saving it.

Doing Right by the Press

Doing right by the press is the third factor. The key is to accept responsibility for relationships with the press, and not delegate it to a PR agency or your internal flacks. Anyway, the press considers PR agencies and internal flacks a hindrance to the pursuit of truth and timeliness.

In fact, when a PR agency's pitch is that they "have all the contacts," run for the door. You can't buy and sell press relationships like baseball cards. You, not your agency, are responsible for personal relationships with the press. Here are ways to do right by the press:

1 ▶ Build the relationship before you need it. Suppose you're working for a big-deal company like Apple. Everyone is calling you for favors. You've got an army of Regettes[1] and a phalanx of Apple PR people. An editor calls you to borrow a Macintosh or to get a copy of *Inside Macintosh*. Big deal, right? Tell him to buy them like everyone else.

Wrong. Help the press before you need it. When you need it, it's too late. Someday you won't be a high-saluting Apple executive, you won't have any power, and you're going to need help. That's when you'll need to call in the favors that you've already dealt out.

The press may pay you back in ways you never imagined. My wife wanted to run in the *San Francisco Examiner's* Bay to Breakers race but missed the deadline. We had been dating a short time, so I seized this opportunity to impress her by contacting Will Hearst III, the publisher of the *Examiner*, and asking him to extend the deadline.

He did. She was impressed. More importantly, so were her parents. Later I repaid the favor by showing him a Macintosh II before any other journalist in the United States. The Apple PR police never knew the difference.

2 ▶ Don't try to manipulate the press. Good reporters and editors are fiercely independent, and they don't consider themselves pawns to be manipulated by you or your agency. The best example of this is *MacWEEK*; it will take on anyone on anything. If you run an even and honest keel, the press will be a lot kinder when the chips are down.

In October, 1988, a Macintosh software company sold its electronic mail product to a competitor. Laurie Flynn of *Info-World* heard about the sale from employees in both companies (that's her job, after all). She called the president of the company who was selling the electronic mail product to verify the story. He denied that the rumors were true: "That's ridic-

---

1. "Regettes" is an affectionate and sadistic term for account executives from a famous Silicon Valley PR agency called Regis McKenna, Inc. Typically, they wear Laura Ashley suits and one week after graduating from college with a BA in Fine Arts, they tell t-shirt clients how to sell their products. If you ever meet someone who has a friend at Regis McKenna, the conversation always starts like this: "I have a friend at Regis McKenna, but she's not like the rest of them."

ulous....Why would we sell off one of our best Macintosh products?" Laurie didn't run the story because she believed him and because her sources told her that the deal wasn't signed yet.

A few weeks later she called him back because she heard that the papers were signed. He denied it again, but she ran the story anyway because she knew he was lying. Less than 24 hours later, his flack called Laurie to set up a formal interview to discuss the sale of the product. He may have delayed the story, but Laurie will never trust him again.

It is un-American to deceive the press, and the president of the company selling the electronic mail product crossed the line. The press is made up of hardworking and ethical people who don't get paid very much. Few errors are malicious or intentional. The president should have confirmed the story and asked Laurie not to print it yet, or responded with "no comment," which is a comment but not manipulation.

3 ▸ Show a little common courtesy. Return phone calls from editors and reporters promptly. Make time on your schedule to meet them. Get to know them as people. Be honest with them. Consistent doses of common courtesy do a lot more than shrimp-and-caviar press conferences and fancy press kits. Make it easy to do business with your company.

Exercise

Call your company and ask for a press kit.

---

4 ▸ Give the press some stories. The goal of giving the press stories is to make yourself such a good source that the press will never burn you. I don't mean giving the press a copy of Apple's unreleased product specs, but you will hear stories that the press can use.

MacWEEK gives you coffee mugs for stories that they run in their rumor column, "Mac the Knife." It's been a personal goal of mine to have the largest collection of *MacWEEK* mugs this side of the Apple exec staff. I have five right now.

However, if you are under a non-disclosure agreement, shut up and honor it. It's a small world, and word will get out that you cannot be trusted. Doubt me? Suppose you violated a non-disclosure and leaked to Amanda Hixson (*Personal Computing*), Maggie Canon and Stephen Mann (*Macintosh Today*), or Mary Fallon and Lisa Raleigh (*San Jose Mercury News*). Today they are all Apple employees.

5 ▶ Treat every press relationship like a long-term investment. The reporter from the *Mountain View Times* may become the next west coast editor of *Business Week*. Or he could go to work for Apple as an evangelist in charge of seeding prototypes. Not only that, but large, national magazines often get story ideas from smaller, local publications. Take the time to educate the press, no matter who they work for at the time, by meeting with them and providing tutorial instructions in your product.

6 ▶ Don't ignore or abuse freelancers. Many of the stories that get published actually originate with freelance writers. They're out there in the world scouting up news and new products, and they pitch interesting angles to their editors. Editors only have so much energy and even less imagination, so they're always looking for good story ideas from their stables of freelancers.

In fact, a good way to get your story in the back door is to get a regular contributor to pitch it for you. If you are really smooth, try to find someone who already loves your product to pitch a review to a magazine.

PR Smarts

The fourth factor is PR smarts. Luck and PR agencies have little to do with good press because it's something that you have to work on all the time to get right.

1 ► Broaden your horizons. Many of the best quotes and metaphors pop out of subjects totally unrelated to your industry. My best sources are the Bible, church sermons, works like *The Art of War* by Sun Tzu, and violent movies. The title for the first chapter of this book, "First Blood," came from a novel by David Morrel which became a Sylvester Stallone movie. "Let a thousand flowers bloom" came from Mao. "Spreading seeds" came from Luke 8:1–15.

Exercise

What did Arnold Schwarzenegger say when he found out that the monster in Predator was bleeding?

A. "Poor thing. Let's call 911."

B. "If it bleeds, we can kill it."

C. "It'll be back."

D. "Quite frankly, I don't give a damn."

---

2 ► Read voraciously. Nothing is more flattering to a reporter than telling him that you read his last article or review, so read the industry rags voraciously. You might learn something, and you'll certainly score points with the reporter. I often tell Denise Caruso that I buy the *San Francisco Examiner* every Sunday only to read her column all the time. And it's true.

3 ▸ Don't hurry to go "on the record." You don't have to answer a reporter's question in real time. When you're in treacherous waters—for example, "What do you think of Apple's latest reorganization?"—tell the reporter that you'll call back after you've thought about it. Then you have time to figure out which "latest reorganization" he was asking about.

4 ▸ Chalk up credit. Whenever the press calls, there is a strong temptation to give them a juicy quote to get your name in print. Other than to impress your parents (or your future wife's parents), there is little reason to say something outrageous to get a little mention in *Business Week* or *The Wall Street Journal*.

It's better to go "off the record" and provide real information "as background." Then you can safely explain what's really going on, and the press will appreciate your insight and candor. The goal is to chalk up a lot of credit so that someday you won't be a quote, you'll be the whole story. Make sure, however, that the reporter or editor has agreed to keep your name out of the story before you start talking.

5 ▸ Find out which way the winds are blowing. Answer a reporter's initial questions with, "What do you think?" and "What are other people saying?" This will give you an initial reading on the situation so you can tell where you stand. You may decide to shut up.

6 ▸ Give away too many samples. It is better to err in the direction of giving away too many samples of your product to the press than too few. It is difficult to decide who is really a reviewer and who is trying to get a freebie, but if you are in doubt, give away too many copies.

The cost of a review copy is a pittance compared to the number of copies a good review can sell. Even a low-circulation publication that is correctly targeted can have great results. *BCS Update,* the Boston Computer Society magazine, for example, goes to the power elite of personal computing.

When You Are Wronged

Every once in a while, the press will wrong you. Typically it happens in a product review. For most people, buying products based on reviews is like picking a spouse based on a beauty contest. The categories—swimsuit, talent, and evening gown—provide some comparisons of the contestants, but they bear little relevance to the qualities that make a happy marriage. Not only that, but you have to rely on a nearsighted panel of judges.

Justice is not done, and it's no wonder. The reviewers have three weeks to review five products in 1,000 words and get paid $500. Then some editor[1] butchers the review they submit. Readers don't get useful analyses. Companies don't get accurate reviews. Editors get angry letters. Reviewers get hostile phone calls.

Bad reviews are bound to happen, and there's little you can do to prevent it (except help pick the reviewer). How should you react to a bad review? I used to think that you should boil the reviewer like a crabb, but I've mellowed some. When you've been wronged, the press feels badly too, and it's your duty to raise hell but do it in an even-handed way. The key is not to roll over, but to deliver a rebuke in a fair manner. The press can take the heat—especially if you have a solid personal relationship with them.

There are two effective methods to raise hell. First, call up the author of the story and his editor and coldly point out where the story is wrong. Appeal to their guilt—after all, they misinformed their readers. Secondly, tell their advertising salesman that you are upset—not because of the "bad" press but

---

1. "An editor is one who separates the wheat from the chaff and prints the chaff." —Adlai Stevenson

because of the "inaccuracies." Advertising and editorial are usually quite separate, but if you have been wronged, the line becomes fuzzy.

A letter to the editor correcting mistakes or protesting unfairness is unwise because it calls more attention to the problem and prolongs the damage. The fewer people who know about the article the better. Go for damage control not public revenge.

An alternative, if you're a gambler, is to ask your loyal customers to write into the magazine for you. When Don Crabb wrote a bad review[1] of 4th Dimension in *InfoWorld*, he received over 400 letters of disagreement from our customers. (Okay, he got some that agreed too). Let your customers defend you. It's much more credible.

The Right Press Conference

High-tech press conferences are all identical these days. They're held in a swanky New York or San Francisco hotel. All the reporters and editors are bribed to attend with shrimp and cheap white wine. The president of the company stands up, fidgets with the slide projector for five minutes, and then gives a 45-minute company overview. Next the product manager gets up and does a demo that crashes twice.

The big moment is next. A figurehead like an Apple vice-president or industry pundit struts up to the podium. He banters on for 15 minutes using words like "strategic," "partnership," "powerful," "innovative," and "graphic." (And your product is a mouse pad.)

Don't use figureheads anymore. They're overused, and the press isn't stupid. They've seen Apple executives proclaim the last five desktop publishing programs and a port of a DOS CAD package without a Macintosh interface as "great." The only reason (shrimp and wine from hotel catering departments aren't that good) that the press attends these press conferences

---

1. Don told me that the editor butchered the review he submitted, and that he didn't assign the numerical score. Still, it was good for his soul to get all those letters.

is for the chance to corner a Steve Jobs or John Sculley for a few minutes. It's not to see your product.

If your product is great, you don't need to validate it with a figurehead. You may not even need a press conference. Let your product do the talking, and let the customers decide.

Working with the Mothership

Love your neighbour, yet don't pull down your hedge.
Benjamin Franklin

Motherships

This chapter explains the right way to work with motherships like Apple, DEC, Sony, or IBM. Motherships are usually the companies that started an industry or currently dominate it. Because of their size, they can frequently determine the success or failure of smaller companies in the industry.

When you run with the elephants, however, you can get trampled, so be careful. This chapter is about Macintosh software developers working with the Mothership Apple, but these skills can be applied to motherships in most high-technology industries.

Understand Apple's Motivation

The key to working with Apple is assuming that its day-to-day motivation is to sell more Macintoshes. Apple does have lofty and noble goals like improving the productivity of its customers, but don't think of it as a magic kingdom with young Marxists sitting around in bean-bag chairs wearing Birkenstocks and discussing the empowerment of the individual. This is a Fortune 500 killing machine that exists to increase the wealth of its shareholders. If you can help its shareholders, you might get some help for yourself.

Exercise

Obtain an Apple annual report. Skip all the body copy, photographs, and graphics and read the income statement.

Identify the Right Part

Much of the difficulty of dealing with Apple is caused by people thinking there is only one company. There are really three Apples: 1) Apple Products, 2) Sales and Marketing, and 3) The Field.[1] They might as well be three different companies, and each of them requires a different approach.

As of May, 1989, Apple Products is headed by Jean-Louis Gassée. This Apple is responsible for research, product development, and manufacturing. Any part of Apple that Gassée runs is product- and technology-oriented. Apple Products wants to see products and technology. They are not concerned with slick marketing and advertising programs so much as your product, technology, your loyalty to Macintosh, and your hatred of Microsoft and IBM.

As of May, 1989, Sales and Marketing and The Field are

---

1. Of this I am quite certain: by the time you read this book, this organizational structure will have changed.

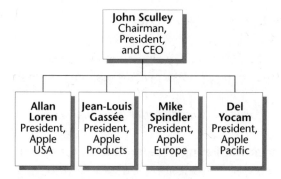

both parts of Apple USA, which is headed by Allan Loren. Allan Loren is relatively new to Apple, and he's going to provide tough, adult supervision to the Cub Scouts. He's been chartered with improving Apple's customer service, and two very good signs are that he has a Nordstrom shopping bag displayed on the wall in his office, and the desktop on his Macintosh has Nordstrom, L.L. Bean, Federal Express, and Apple logos. He also owns two Mont Blanc pens.

Exercise

A man went to a Hyundai dealership and bought a car. When he got home, he read his manual and found out that his $8,000 car had a 36,000-mile, 36-month warranty. Later, he went to an Apple dealer and bought a Macintosh II and a LaserWriter NTX for $10,000. When he got home, he read his manual and found out that his new computer equipment had a 90-day warranty.

What can explain this?

A. *A car is driven every day, it is subject to road wear, rain, sleet, and snow, and it has thousands of moving parts. A computer sits on a desk.*

B. *The finance department of Apple calculated that earnings*

> *would go down if Apple extended the warranty period.*
>
> C. *The sales department of Apple has been unable to prove that extending the warranty period would lead to more sales.*
>
> D. *Hyundai cars are made better than Apple computers.*

Sales and Marketing is responsible for the overall sales, marketing, and support functions at the Cupertino headquarters. It wants to sell more Macs in the next 90 days, and is obsessed with quarterly sales and earnings. It is made up of sales and marketing types who work in City Center II (Apple engineers call the building "Ego Center II"). They are impressed by flashy marketing, and they love presentations using words like "platform," "SQL," "connectivity," "desktop," "networking," "channel," and "infrastructure." They think that HyperCard is a database.

The Field includes more than 50 sales offices and 1,500 salespeople throughout the United States. They do battle in the trenches every day, so they need ways to differentiate Macintosh from the IBM PC. There is no connection between Sales and Marketing in Cupertino (the corporate pukes) and The Field, so don't assume that connections at the headquarters have any bearing on your success in the field. Go after each part independently.

Reorgs

To work with Apple you must understand reorganizations. You used to be able to predict who would advance in Apple by what they drank—alfalfa juice (Jobs), beer (Campbell), and blood (Gassée). It's not so simple anymore. At great risk, I will answer the most commonly whispered question: "Why does Apple reorganize so often?" The answers are applicable to many high-growth companies.

First, rapid growth makes reorganizations necessary. Apple almost tripled sales revenue between 1984 and 1988 from $1.5 billion to $4 billion. This kind of growth causes great stress on systems, structures, and employees and antiquates them very quickly. Thus, reorganizations must occur.

Secondly, Apple is a very political place. Often decisions are made on the basis of what's politically acceptable, not what's right. Thus, organizations are thrown together in curious ways so that everyone can have his own sandbox. This is very different from the Jobs days, when he had the biggest sandbox with the most toys, and you were either allowed to play in it or watch from the classroom.

Thirdly, Apple cannot pull the trigger and fire people. People and their organizations are shifted perpetually as they screw up. No one ever gets fired from Apple because accountability is not an Apple value. Even after an employee resigns, he is typically hired back as a consultant at three times the old salary. If a high-level executive leaves, Apple forgives the house loan that it gave him to quit IBM.

Apple employees have grown to accept reorganizations, and you will have to also. The saying around Cupertino is, "If you don't like this reorg, don't worry. There'll be another one in 90 days." Mark my words, organizational stability is the most serious issue facing Apple today.

Exercise

In 1988, some middle managers of a company had as many as six supervisors. What could explain this?

A. *The executive staff learned how to use MacDraw and went nuts.*

B. *The company wanted to get closer to the customer.*

C. *The company believed that exposure to a diversity of management styles stimulates employees.*

D. *The VP of marketing changed again.*

Beggars Can't be Choosers

Now that I've explained Apple's motivation and organization, let's examine how to work with Apple. First, smart Macintosh developers have accepted the fact that they are beggars on Apple's doorstep. When I left Apple I knew that I would have to grovel for prototypes and co-marketing like everyone else. I even had to apply for certification.

There are over 10,000 Apple certified developers, and there are about 20 evangelists to help them. This ratio of developers

 April 16, 1987

Guy Kawasaki
Acius, Inc.
141 California Ave. B304
Palo Alto, CA 94306

Dear Mr. Kawasaki:

After a careful review of your application, I am pleased to announce your selection as a Certified Apple Developer. Congratulations!

Certification is for a period of 18 months. After 18 months you will be notified to update us on the status of your products.

We at Developer Services are committed to providing you with timely information and assistance to further your product development and company's success. As a Certified Developer you will receive our developer newsletter and various information on existing programs and seminars. You will also be eligible to purchase development equipment at a discount.

Being a Developer, you may require technical support. You may send your questions to our technical staff via US Mail or MCI Mail. The MCI Mail addresses for technical support are MACTECH for Macintosh and DTS for Apple // concerning development questions. For more information on obtaining this service please contact MCI directly at (800) MCI-MAIL.

You may wish to consider applying to our Registered Developer Program. An application and explanation letter are enclosed for your review.

We are delighted to welcome you to the Certified Developer Program. I fully expect that you and Apple will enjoy a close and successful working relationship. Should you have any questions, please contact Developer Services at (408) 973-4897 or MCI Mail address: Apple (Certified Developers).

Sincerely,

Farida Benderradji
Certified Developer Program

to evangelists indicates the level of support you can reasonably expect from Apple.

Apple is past the stage where breakthrough software will garner heavy support. The first and only time this happened was with PageMaker, but Apple was on the ropes then, and Paul Brainerd had the smelling salts. If you don't believe me, ask Steve Wolfram. He created a symbolic mathematics software product called Mathematica that could open up as many markets for Macintosh as PageMaker. He's getting nothing out of the ordinary from Apple. Interestingly enough, Steve Jobs is bundling Mathematica with his machine.

Secondly, be realistic about the potential impact your product can have and therefore the amount of support you can reasonably expect. A shoot-em-up game for the Macintosh II, for example, will not get much attention because Apple doesn't position Macintosh IIs as game machines. A connectivity product that links Macintoshes and mainframes will get a lot of support.

Thirdly, don't let Apple or any other company determine your success or failure because this is not Apple's responsibility. Macintosh developers dream about Apple parting the ocean for them. Apple not only won't make the ocean part; it couldn't even if it tried. If any Apple employee tells you differently, then the employee is either a summer hire or someone with the word "strategic"[1] in his title. Neither will be around long.

Still, Apple has the best third-party developer programs and support services of any hardware manufacturer. More than any other manufacturer, Apple recognizes that developers are a key to its future success. More than any other hardware company, Apple truly appreciates and respects its third-party developers. Apple dedicates over 150 people and spends over $20 million per year to support developers. That's about 140 people and $18 million more than any other company.

For example, Apple helps babyships in four ways, and

---

1. When "strategic" is in a person's title, it means that the person really doesn't have a job. Steve Scheier, Allan Loren's special assistant, decided to change his business cards after he read a manuscript of this book because they said "Manager of Strategic Projects." Now they say "Assistant to the President."

Apple's practices can be applied to other industries. The four ways are:

1 ▶ Providing generic assistance to anyone that asks politely. Developer Services and Developer Co-Marketing help Apple certified developers promote products to user groups, dealers, national accounts, and other developers. You can also buy equipment at a 50 percent discount. For about $500, Apple will send out your product brochures to over 1,000 user groups.

2 ▶ Blessing twenty to forty products as "strategic." A blessed product gets featured in the Apple trade show booths, included in dealer mailings, and featured in Apple and dealer training classes. These activities can have enormous impact on the sales of your product. You achieve this status by demonstrating how your product can sell more Apple hardware and by following the rules of the Apple road in the next section.

3 ▶ Sanctifying a handful of products. Excel and PageMaker are two products in this category. The effort required to achieve this status and the probability of it occurring make it a foolish pursuit. Apple only does this when it's desperate, but desperate days are over until the next new computer. You cannot achieve this status so don't waste your time trying. In the end, only the customer can sanctify your product and line your pocket with money.

4 ▶ Seeding with prototypes. One of the most important things that Apple provides is prototypes of its products. The most commonly asked questions are, "Who gets seeded?" and "Why?" Let me explain how Apple handles this process. Other motherships handle the process in similar ways.

Prior to the introduction of a new computer, Apple seeds what it considers strategic organizations. The first prototypes are made by hand and used for testing by engineers. The factory eventually delivers several hundred preproduction prototypes that are allocated to evangelism, national accounts, VARs, and other Apple channels.

The evangelists distribute their allocation like precious gems because they are evaluated on their ability to get products that ship at the introduction of a new computer. Demos, announcements, and intentions don't count for much. There are three categories of developers who get the first units:

1 ▸ The companies that don't matter. Unfortunately, some prototypes go to the big-name MS-DOS companies because Apple thinks that they give Macintosh credibility. These units are wasted: pearls before swine. Fortunately, these companies can be counted on one hand.

2 ▸ The big companies that matter. Companies like Aldus and Microsoft are sure seeds—Aldus because of its role in the history of desktop publishing, Microsoft because it has two very long needles in Apple's arm called Word and Excel. (Apple is afraid that Macintosh is not a legitimate computer without Microsoft products). In general, Apple seeds these kinds of companies because it is afraid that reports of bugs in major software products will hurt the sales of Macintosh.

3 ▸ The companies that need it—gutsy visionaries. These companies need prototypes because they are creating specific products for a particular Macintosh. A company developing a color paint program or software that uses the 68881,[1] for example, was sure to get a Macintosh II.

Sometimes even gutsy visionaries who need prototypes don't get them. CE Software, one of the small, great Macintosh developers (they created ten Macintosh products including SideKick, DiskTop, and QuickKeys), got seeded once with a Macintosh prototype in five years of Macintosh development. During that time, they should have gotten prototypes of the

1. A 68881 is a coprocessing chip that speeds up mathematical calculations for a computer. I don't know why high-tech companies can't seem to come up with sexier names like "TBMC"—Top Banana Math Chip.

Macintosh 512K, Macintosh Plus, Macintosh 512Ke, Macintosh II, and Macintosh IIcx. The only time CE got seeded, it was because they were doing a product for Borland.

Rules of the Apple Road

Here are the rules for negotiating the road paved by Apple:

1 ▶ Match your product to their current marketing thrust. When the six-color elephant rumbles, jump on his back. If Apple is going after desktop publishing, tie your product (whether it's true or not) to the publishing market—not the vast potential market made up of cartoonists.

Mindscape published a product named ComicWorks that was developed by MacroMind and comic book artist Mike Saenz. Because it had a lot of graphic features that no other program offered, Mindscape also packaged it as GraphicWorks to go after the desktop publishing market. It almost worked.

Exercise

What is the difference between a company calling a market "communications" and "desktop communications?"

A. Desktop communications is prettier.

B. Desktop communications has more margin.

C. The company wants co-marketing.

---

2 ▶ Find a champion for your product. Find one person to tuck you under his wing and act as your evangelist. Things get so mucked up in Cupertino that everyone looking out for you means that no one is looking out for you. John Scull (no, not John Sculley) was the champion of desktop publishing for Apple. He managed the efforts of Apple's marketing, training, and field sales personnel and coordinated them with Aldus' own activities. His clear identification as the desktop publishing champion was a large factor in Aldus' and desktop publishing's success.

3 ► Don't take no for an answer. There are at least five organizations at Apple that can help a developer: Developer Services, Evangelism, Field Sales, Developer Co-Marketing, and Business Marketing (or Education Marketing depending on your product). They don't communicate well with each other, so if one group says no, keep asking until you find one that says yes. It's like asking Mom if Dad says no.

4 ► Take whatever you can get whenever you can get it. Apple usually reorganizes every two to three months so your champion may not be able to help you a quarter from now. If Apple offers you something, take it and be thankful. I once got called at 6:10 PM to show 4th Dimension the next day at 10:00 AM at an Apple sneak preview of the Macintosh IIcx. I was annoyed to find out so late, but it was better than another database company going in our place.

5 ► Don't approach Apple as if you are going to save it. I heard this pitch ten times a week when I was in charge of Evangelism. It didn't work then. It certainly won't work now. All you'll do is antagonize people. Do a product only if you will profit by it—not because you think you're doing Apple a favor. Wolfram tried this approach on Apple with Mathematica. If you ever meet him, ask him what happened.

6 ► Don't threaten Apple. Let's face it—few companies have the clout to pull this off. No single software product can make or break Macintosh at this point. The only company that came close to successfully threatening Apple is Microsoft. In 1986 Bill Gates told Apple that he would consider stopping Macintosh development if Apple pursued a copyright infringement suit[1]

---

1. A copyright infringement suit is a way to create confusion in the marketplace until your engineering staff can get its act together. Typically, it occurs after it's

against Microsoft. Apple backed down because of the importance of Word and Excel to Macintosh. Temporarily, anyway. There is no doubt that Bill Gates can produce testosterone, and that's another reason that Microsoft is such a great company.

Exercise

Write a high-end word processor and spreadsheet for the NeXT machine. Clone the look and feel[1] of the NeXT machine for another computer. See if NeXT sues you.

---

too late so that the plaintiff looks like the bad guy and the defendant looks like the good guy.

1. "Look and feel" refers to the visual appearance of a product. Typically, it is invented by one company, copied by a second company, and reaped by a third. The second company then institutes a copyright infringement suit against the third company. If Sun Tzu were alive today, he'd call it "The War of Art."

How to Give Good Demo

Every crowd has a silver lining.
P.T. Barnum

The Role of a Demo

This chapter explains how to do the right product demonstration. The right demo doesn't cost much, but it can counteract your competitors' marketing and advertising. A great demo informs the audience about your product, communicates the benefits of owning your product, and inspires the audience to take action.

Preparation

The foundation of a great demo is a well-planned and interesting script. A good script is like telling a story: the audience should eagerly and gratefully attend to every word and action. These are the requirements of a good demo script:

1 ▶ Short. A good demo lasts about 30 minutes with an additional ten minutes for Q and A—giving you a total length of 40 to 45 minutes. A demo that lasts longer will tire your audience.

2 ▶ Simple. A good demo is simple and easy to follow. It should communicate no more than one or two key messages. The goal is to show the audience enough to get tantalized but not so much that they get bewildered. The rollout demos of version 2.0 of 4th Dimension concentrated on two messages: improved performance and ease-of-use.

Exercise

Watch a product demo. How many messages did it have?

---

3 ▶ Sweet. A good demo is sweet. It shows the hottest features and differentiates your product from the competition's. You have to show real functionality, though—not flash—or you will disappoint the sailors and The Cult in the audience. Imagine that every time you show a feature someone shouts, "So what?"

4 ▶ Swift. A good demo has a fast pace. Never do anything in a demo that lasts more than 15 seconds. For example, although incredibly impressive, don't show your word processor reformatting a 1,000 page document in a minute. It's far better to repaginate.ten pages instantaneously than 1,000 pages in a minute.

5 ▶ Substantial. Show how your product builds a solution. Customers want to *do* things with your product so they want to know *how* the product works. They are sophisticated, so they realize that with enough work even an IBM PC can produce newsletters, layouts, or databases. Credibility comes from seeing what it takes to create the end result. A good demo shows customers *how* your product helps them. If you do it right, all you may have to worry about is *how many* they order.

Exercise

Write out a demo script in step-by-step detail. Have someone who is not familiar with your product try to perform the script. If he can't do it, your audience will get confused watching the demo.

Getting to Carnegie Hall

The second step is to practice your demo. Then practice some more. Most people think that knowing a product is enough to give a good demo. That's not true—no more so than knowing the words to a song will enable you to sing it. Practice your demo so many times that it looks like you're not even trying. Michael Jackson said it all:

Nobody could duplicate Mr. Astaire's ability, but what I never stop trying to emulate is his total discipline, his absolute dedication to every aspect of his art. He rehearsed, rehearsed, and rehearsed some more, until he got it just the way he wanted it. It was Fred Astaire's work ethic that few people ever discussed and even fewer could ever hope to equal.

The lack of discernible effort is a concept espoused in Castiglione's *Book of the Courtier*. All of these courtly types are sitting around in a castle waiting out the black plague, and they decide to fill the time with a contest. Each person will speak on what characteristics make up a great courtier.

One person gets up and talks about how a great courtier is a wonderful handler of horses. Another talks about strength in arms. Another, gentle speech. And so on. Finally one gets up and says yes, a great courtier must have all these things, but above all he must have *sprezzatura* (nonchalance). He must be a master of all those things but look as if he's not even trying.

Practice your demo until you can do it with nonchalance. Otherwise you belong in the Carnegie Deli, not Carnegie Hall.

Exercise

Which of the five is the best comparison?

Practice is to demo as _____ are to IPOs.

A. Red herrings

B. Ferraris

C. Lawyers

> *D. Prenuptial agreements*
>
> *E. Profits*

At the Performance

I really love to demo because it's like being on stage. I've demoed 4th Dimension to over 10,000 people, and I think that it's one of the most important things that I do. Here are some things that have helped me with my demos.

1 ▶ Circulate with the audience before the demo. Understanding the audience—who they are, where they came from, why they are there—helps you to do a much better demo. Walk through the audience and meet people. The audience will warm up to you because you become a person, not a performer on stage. It also helps you relax because the audience isn't made up of strangers anymore.

If it's not possible to circulate with the audience before the demo, ask some background questions when you get to the podium. "How many of you own Macintoshes?" "How many already own a word processor?" "How many of you have an AppleTalk network?" This will provide you with some information and show the audience that you care about who they are.

2 ▶ Begin by explaining what you are going to do. Do it. Then recap what you've done. A simple introduction like this will help the audience understand what is going to happen and make it easier for them to follow the demo. The recap enables people who got lost during your demo to catch up and understand what you showed. A good opening line is, "If there is one thing that I'd like you to walk away with today, it is..." Repeat the message at the end of the demo.

3 ▶ Get to the demo quickly. Spend no more than five minutes talking about the history of your company and your marketing. The audience is there to see the product, not you. They don't care how much you've spent on your company video either. Skip the crap and get to it.

4 ▶ Be smooth. Jackie Stewart, a famous race car driver, teaches high-performance driving by installing a dish-like object that can hold a ball on the hood of his cars. The goal is to drive the car so smoothly that the ball doesn't roll out. Smoothness wins in demoing too.

Don't lose the audience by going too fast or bore them by going too slowly. One of our salespeople was so jerky in his presentation that I made him practice to a metronome. Smoothness also means that you have a relaxed voice, your attire is orderly, you look like you are having a good time, and you are physically comfortable. Remember, this is a performance!

5 ▶ Don't try to impress people with technical jargon. If you try to impress your audience, you'll lose half of it, and the other half probably knows more than you do. If you want to play it safe, bring a T-shirt to back you up with technical expertise. Introduce the T-shirt to the audience too. This will impress the sailors.

6 ▶ Make eye contact with the audience. Make eye contact with people during your demo. If you pretend that you are doing a demo and talking to a specific person in the audience, it will help you to relax and maintain a comfortable pace. You can't make contact with people in the back row, but they can tell if you are talking *to* the audience or talking *at* the audience.

7 ▶ Interject humor into your demo. Humor is the element that separates a great demonstrator from a good one. An easy and safe target for a Macintosh developer is the IBM PC. Another good target is your own company. If you're an ex-Apple employee, Apple is a good, easy, and big target. (No one loves Apple more than I do so no one can get away with slamming it like I do.)

8 ▶ Control the demo. Don't take questions during the demo because it will break your rhythm and concentration. If someone asks a question from the floor, politely answer it, then say, "I'd like to have questions at the end of the demo so that we can finish on time." The audience will understand.

9 ▶ End with an exclamation point. Finish your demo with the most dazzling sample newsletter, graphic, or feature that you can perform. Make the audience dream of lofty accomplishments and inspire them to run out and buy your product.

If You Crash...

The thought of crashing in a demo enrages me. Macintosh can do most things better than any other computer, and it's true for crashes, too. Sometimes it starts buzzing and popping and flashing and won't stop until you pull the plug. Nothing crashes like a Macintosh.

My most spectacular crash was in front of 800 people at the January 1988 Macworld Expo in San Francisco. I was using MultiFinder[1] and shouldn't have. That's an excuse, and there really is none—either you crash or you don't. With enough practice and preparation, there is no reason ever to crash. You should know exactly how to navigate through your product and avoid all the traps.

If you do crash, try to look calm and keep moving. Give a one-line explanation and go on. I've found that blaming Apple's system software[2] usually works because everyone in the audience can relate.

After the Performance

Interaction with the audience after the demo is as important as the dismount in a gymnastics routine. You can ruin a good

---

1. MultiFinder is system software that Apple provides so that you can crash in more than one application at once.

2. For Apple, system software is what it copied from Xerox PARC. For IBM, system software is whatever Bill Gates says it is. For Xerox PARC, it's whatever they fumbled back in the 1950s.

demo or recover from a bad one with a good after-performance performance. Here's how to finish like a winner:

1 ▶ Open a forum for Q and A. Take every question seriously, and answer the question that is asked. A good rule is: "Ask a silly question, get a serious answer." If you don't know the answer, say so, but don't answer a different question. If you can't answer a question, admit it and ask the T-shirt to answer it, or get the person's business card and get the answer for the person later.

If the question requires a lengthy, technical explanation, ask the person to come see you after the demo so you don't lose the entire audience. Remember that there is no such thing as a stupid question, only a rude presenter.

2 ▶ Don't rush off. After your demo, don't rush off. The people who are really interested in your product may have more questions for you, and your current customers may want to talk to you. Spend a long time with these people because they are the ones who pay your salary.

3 ▶ Do specialized demos. During a presentation, I usually don't do specialized demos like SQL and CL/1[1] because they are relevant to only a few people. Instead I show them after the general demo to people who are interested.

The Rambo Demo

The multiple-vendor shoot-out demo is a special circumstance that is treacherous for any company. Let's say you're at a trade show, and there is a breakout session for Macintosh databases. Omnis, Double Helix II, and 4th Dimension are going to be shown back-to-back. Here's how to play the game:

---

1. SQL is software invented by IBM for the management of large amounts of data. Since it was invented by IBM, everyone except IBM has figured out how to implement it. CL/1 is software invented by Network Innovations to enable Macintoshes to access SQL data. Apple bought Network Innovations because it couldn't figure out what IBM couldn't figure out. The only thing Network Innovations can't figure out is why it sold out. SQL is pronounced "sequel" not "S-Q-L." This is a good way to tell if the person has figured out SQL.

Assess the others' demo skills. If you are the best, you can go either first or last. If you go first, set the pace so that the competition has to play catch-up. If you go last, your amazing demo will be the one that people remember.

If you are in the middle of the pack, go after the competitor with the worst demo skills. This is the easiest time to look good because most audiences will compare you to the demonstrator who preceded you.

If you are the worst, read this chapter over. If you're still the worst, go first and be brief. Going first enables you to have the freshest audience, and the audience cannot compare you to anyone who preceded you. After several products, people will forget who was the biggest bozo.

During your demo, never refer to the competition unless you can wipe the floor with them. If your product is only incrementally better, avoid advertising your competitors. Slamming the competition usually makes you look bad unless it's an MS-DOS company.

Two Last Things

First, have the person who knows the product best, not the highest ranking, do the demo. Just because a vice-president is there doesn't mean he has to do the demo. People who come to demos came to see the product, not some management nitwit.

Secondly, send a thank-you note to the host of your demo. Not many people send a thank-you note. It goes a long way.

Presentation Manager

*Q: If you find so much that is unworthy
of reverence in the United States, then
why do you live here?
A: Why do men go to zoos?*

H. L. Mencken

BFD: Big French Deal

This chapter explains how to do the right presentation to a high-level, technically sophisticated, and arrogant executive like The King: Jean-Louis Gassée. (I asked Jean-Louis to edit the manuscript of this book to make sure I got things right.) These skills are relevant to anyone who makes presentations. "If I can make it there, I can make it anywhere."

As you can tell, Jean-Louis is one of my favorite people and topics. When I worked for Jean-Louis at Apple, he was like an older brother and parole officer to me. He was the kind of older brother who told you not to smoke and not to drink because he had a cough and a hangover. The best parole officer is an ex-con, and the only thing an ex-con respects is power.

Exercise

Go to a jeweler and get your ear pierced. Buy a diamond stud earring. Learn to speak with a French accent. You may be the next president of your company.

As president of Apple Products (after the latest reorganization), he is one of the most powerful people in the Macintosh community. He can make the six-color water lap gently on your bow, or sink you. He and great Macintosh companies gravitate toward each other instinctively.

Inside Gassée

This is the inside scoop on The King and executives like him. The higher you go in a Macintosh Way company, the more you'll find these observations to be true.

1 ► He loves products. He doesn't care about slick marketing or brand-name recognition. If you can get your product into his hands, you have about 30 seconds to win him over. He's not going to read your manuals—he's going to boot your program and go. This is a man who has a disassembled Sony CD player mounted as art in his office.

2 ► He views products as tools, not solutions. A hole is a solution. A drill is a tool. He believes that Apple's role (and yours, too) is to provide tools so that customers can create their own solutions. Never position your product as a solution to him.

Exercise
Go to a hardware store. Ask the clerk how much business they do in carpentry solutions. Then ask how much business they do in carpentry tools.

3 ► He likes products that appeal to both passengers and sailors. Gassée likes products that you can smoke right out of the box or roll your own. He doesn't like products that are easy to use but lack depth. He despises products that frustrate people as they progress up the power curve.

4 ► He's got a case on everyone. He can't help it, he's French.

When you talk to him, slam someone. Anyone. At Apple. In the industry. In politics. Tell him that someone is the Dan Quayle of the industry. The odds are excellent that he thinks that the person is a bozo too, and you will develop instant rapport.

5 ▶ He has no respect for authority. I think that he made me a director knowing that I was leaving Apple because he wanted to wave my resignation around and say, "You see, you can't buy everyone. You blew it with Guy." He told me to get a company Mercedes,[1] drive it once around the Apple parking lot, and give back the keys.

6 ▶ He's a bad enemy. Never go above him or around him. If he says no, back down, regroup, then approach him again. Telling him that you'll "go to Sculley" will sink you. I'll share with you a little Gassée story that illustrates this.

Ed Esber went around Esther Dyson's computer conference (the same one I told you about in the first chapter) bragging that he was going to drill Jean-Louis a new orifice because Apple was

---

1. A Mercedes is a management perquisite at Apple. Typically, four to five senior-level executives leave Apple each year, so if you know the human resources person who handles the car leases, it is possible to get very good deals on Mercedes, Jaguars, BMWs, and once, an Allanté.

going to publish Silver Surfer. Because I was a loyal employee, I made sure Jean-Louis knew that Ed was redesigning his anatomy.

About a year later Ashton-Tate printed a brochure for Byline, a PC desktop publishing product. The brochure said, "Because Byline works the way you do, you don't have to waste time with a mouse or learning a Macintosh-like graphics environment." I sent a copy of the brochure to Jean-Louis with a note that said, "Looks like Ed also writes ad copy when he's not rearranging your anatomy."

Jean-Louis, bless his little French heart, took my note and the brochure and sent it to Esber. He added his own note that said, "I just wanted you to know that Guy is keeping me informed of your activities." Look who's got an extra orifice.

Close Encounters of the French Kind

Suppose that you get an appointment with Jean-Louis or a Jean-Louis clone. Your problems are about to begin unless your presentation is well thought out. What are you asking him to do? Why should he do it? How much will it cost? When do you need it?

Kyle Mashima issued guidelines about meeting with Jean-Louis to his employees. Combining Kyle's rules and my own experience, here are the most important rules for a Jean-Louis presentation:

1 ▶ Make a presentation that he couldn't. If he doesn't learn anything from your presentation, you can quiche the meeting goodbye. And don't try to flatter him by repeating what he said at a prior meeting—he was probably jerking the attendees around and isn't going to be impressed by getting his malarkey fed back to him.

2 ▶ Layer your presentation. He enjoys presentations that are layered—double-click[1] on the top level, explain, double-click

---

1. Double-click refers to the action of clicking twice with a Macintosh mouse. Typically, a double-click starts an action. It is the reason that most Macintosh owners have calluses on their forefingers.

To: PM's
Fr: Kyle
Re: Close Encounters of the French Kind
Dt: March 19, 1987

Here are some guidelines for preparing for a Jean-Louis presentation. This could save your life. These are industrial skills - not for use at home.

Rules:

• Don't get stuck on your presentation pitch. Listen and respond. Stop using your slides when it's clear that their not relevant (look for signals from me or Guy - ie: eye brows and coughing).

• If you make changes that JLG requests, you may have not done your job right the first time - otherwise, why are these changes necessary.

• Never hand out a copy of your presentation before hand - he reads ahead and you'll lose control.

• Never use all CAPS in your slides. Hard to read and dumb with all of our incredible technology.

• Never read what's on the slide. He can read too! You should talk around the concept of the slide and add color.

• Don't insult his intelligence by pointing out obvious things - ie: the Macintosh interface is considered superior to the MS-DOS environment. Better to make a quick statement not on a slide like , "you know that our interface is superior, therefore ....."

• Use uncluttered, clear graphics whenever possible. Shows clear thinking.

• Analogies are good but dangerous. Use them wisely. Vague metaphors are great. He uses them all the time.

• Being too technical at the right time is okay. Out teching him is a good way to show your depth of understanding.

• Avoid arguments. If there isn't agreement quickly, try another tact or move on.

• Stay focused on your objectives. Don't stray. Start out presentation with what you're trying to accomplish. Wrap up meeting with short summary of agreements and action items.

• Always address questions that have been asked in a timely manner or make sure that he no longer cares.

• Make your presentation clean, crisp and precise. You don't need a lot of dressing. It won't impress him.

• Remember to answer the "what" and the "how". *What is it* and *how does it do it*.

• Do the dramatic stuff at the beginning - otherwise, you may never get to it.

• Don't feel bad. Most times you've made significant progress and you won't know it until an hour after the presentation.

on the next level, explain, etc. This kind of presentation keeps him interested and increases his respect for your bandwidth.

3 ► Don't give him a copy of your presentation at the beginning of the meeting. If you give him a copy of the presentation, he will read ahead, and you'll lose control of the meeting. Also, giving him the presentation provides him extra time to think of objections.

4 ▶ Simplify your overheads. Overheads should contain a minimum amount of text so that he must listen to you. For example, a good overhead contains positioning as a bullet item ("• Positioning") instead of text that says, "The positioning of 4th Dimension is the most powerful database for a personal computer."

Bullet items are better than sentences or phrases because they provide a framework or clue that you can talk around. An overhead should contain no more than five bullet items because a properly structured presentation will not have any topics with more than five important points.

Exercise

Examine your overheads. How many contain complete sentences? How many contain more than five bullet points? How many of your proposals have been approved lately?

---

5 ▶ Bullet speak. Talk in bullets—short, simple phrases that specifically address each point. Long, waxing, and philosophical orations have no place in a presentation to Jean-Louis. When you are long-winded, Jean-Louis is thinking, "What is he trying to hide?"

6 ▶ Be flexible. You may have a carefully rehearsed presentation, but if he wants to shuck and jive, be prepared and willing to change. Interpreting his desire to diverge is tricky: he's either already bought off on your presentation or he doesn't agree and is getting bored.

7 ▶ Do the dramatic stuff first. If Jean-Louis doesn't like the beginning of your presentation, he may throw you out. So get to the dramatic stuff right away. You may never have the chance to show him the great stuff if it's late in the meeting.

8 ▶ Never tell him that anyone likes your product. *"InfoWorld* thinks this is the best port of an MS-DOS program they've ever seen," is not a good way to start a meeting with Jean-Louis. He probably thinks that the person or organization you mentioned is a total bozo and telling him that a bozo likes your product is not a good idea. A better idea is to tell him that people cannot understand your product—affirming Jean-Louis' opinion that most people are bozos. The best idea is to shut up and let Jean-Louis decide for himself.

9 ▶ Show him how to build. He likes to see the *how* not the *what* of a product because he is a technologist at heart. Show him how to build a database or a newsletter, not the finished result. Don't ever use VideoWorks or HyperCard to show him what your product does.

10 ▶ Don't let him drive your product. Jean-Louis takes great pride in his ability to crash software. You have little to gain and a lot to lose by letting your pigeon drive. In February, 1989 I showed version 2.0 of 4th Dimension to Jean-Louis and John Sculley on Jean-Louis' Macintosh.

The high point of the meeting for Jean-Louis was when I crashed. He remarked, "Ah, my reputation is preserved." When I reopened the sample database, it was still intact, and I told them that I had wanted to show 4th Dimension's "data integrity." Jean-Louis laughed and kicked my chair—I did learn from the best.

11 ▶ Take whatever he says literally. Every word that he says is there for a reason, and you have to take him very literally. Here are some translations to help you understand what he is really saying:

Gassée Speak	Localized to American
"Your product has potential."	Your product is crap. Every product has potential, no matter how little.

"I will try to think of ways to help you."	He will *try* and he will *think*— as opposed to do. He hasn't promised to actually *do* anything.
"Your product will sell."	If one copy sells, he was right. He's not predicting that it's the next 1-2-3.
"Your product could be even better."	Why are you wasting my time with this crap?

Exercise

Practice using the word "even" to insult people. Your car could be "even" better. Your children could be "even" smarter. Your book could be "even" more interesting. Your earring could have an "even" bigger diamond.

---

12 ▶ Don't argue with him. Try a different angle, move on to another topic, or change the demo. A good game to play is to feign agreement, then whipsaw him. For example, if he tells you that your product has a confusing interface, come back with: "Jean-Louis, I agree with you. The interface can be improved, but it shows the richness of our product and that we have many powerful features. How would you redesign it?" You aren't going to win a frontal attack. In football, the best pass rusher runs around an offensive blocker, not over him, even if he has to slap the blocker's head.

13 ▶ Use metaphors. He loves to use metaphors—especially sexual and military ones. The vaguer the better. He uses metaphors to blow past people while they try to figure them out. (When Jean-Louis edited this section, his comment was, "I disagree. I use metaphors because a) I like the shock of words and b) they help convey the difficult or downright ineffable.")

You can believe me or you can believe him. In either case, if he uses a metaphor, just nod, smile, laugh, and act like you understand him whether you do or not. Describe your product as "a beautiful woman going to war," and he'll give you anything you want.

Exercise

Use the following insults on your enemies:

His elevator doesn't make it to the penthouse.

His receiver is off the hook.

His oil doesn't reach his dipstick.

If brains were dynamite, he couldn't blow his hat off.

Fiber brings out the best in him.

---

14 ▶ Shut up when you've got the sale. If he agrees with you, make him sign on the dotted line, shut up, and get out of his office quickly.

By the Way

If you are going to put his name on an overhead, get "Gassée" right. The "é" is obtained by pressing the Option key and "e" then "e" again. And it's the first "e." And you don't pronounce the "s" in Jean-Louis. Pretend that you are presenting to Jean-Louis and maybe someday Jean-Louis will be presenting to you.

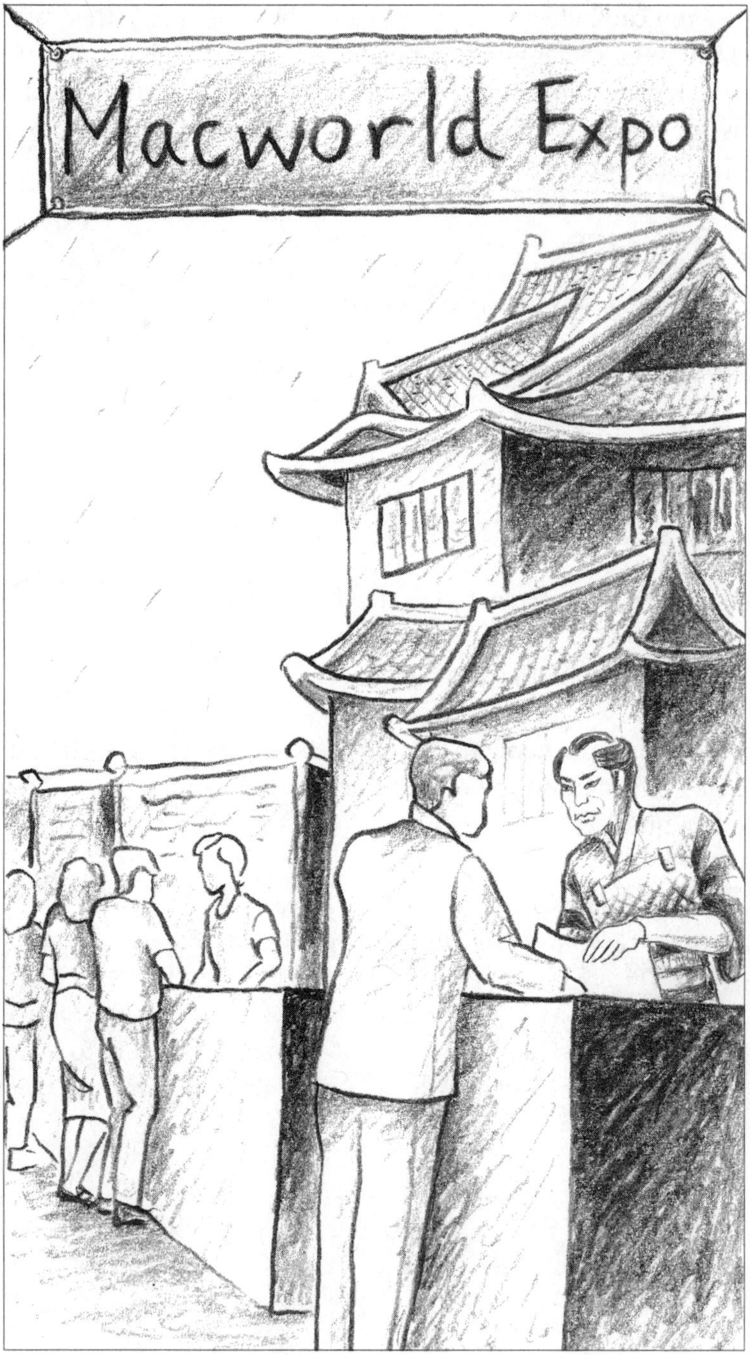
Macworld Expo

Trade Show Mavenship

It is only the shallow people who do not judge by appearance.

Oscar Wilde

Doing Trade Shows Right

This chapter explains how to do trade shows right and get the right information into the hands of the right people—thousands at a time. Trade shows seem like total anarchy, but there is a science to them.

Booths

Booths are a rip-off. For the price of a house (except in California), companies will make you a booth that you'll use eight days a year. The system tries to convince you to spend a lot of money on a booth by making you feel paranoid or guilty. "You do want to impress your customers, don't you?" "Your competition built a more expensive booth." "This booth will last for years." You will get ripped off, but at least you can optimize your booth.

1 ▶ Create a large presentation area. The more people that can watch your presentation, the more effective your booth. A projector or large screen monitor with a PA system that will drown out your competitors are musts. Aldus has an area in their booth full of Macintosh IIs where users can sit down and go through the product demo with an instructor.

2 ▸ Take the aisles. Design your booth so that when the presentation area is filled, the audience is forced into the aisles. This has several advantages. You get some floor space for free. Your booth will always look like it was "overflowing the aisles." And your competition will get psyched out. When you walk past an Aldus booth and see a crowd in the aisles plus a packed demo area, you have to conclude Aldus has a hot product.

3 ▸ Pick a spot near the mothership. Motherships usually radiate an aura. You want to be bathed in it. The mothership always draws a crowd, so being close to it helps your booth traffic too. It's also a lot easier to describe your booth location as "right by the Apple booth" than "booth 2198."

4 ▸ Coordinate with your product packaging. Packaging, marketing materials, and a booth that tie together produce more "impressions" that reinforce your company image. This makes you look larger and more established than you really are. Silicon Beach Software doesn't coordinate its packaging with its booth, but it does coordinate its aloha shirts with its booth. If it works, go with it.

5 ▸ Build in flexibility. Create a booth that can grow as your trade show needs grow. Instead of building a new booth every six months, pick a design that enables you to add more modules. Also, a modular booth can be used for smaller shows by taking only a part of it.

6 ▸ Allocate an area for your developers. The presence of developers in your trade show booth is convincing evidence that your company and product are successful. Developers in your booth *shows* that you are successful so that you don't have to *say* you are. They also reduce your staffing requirements, which reduces your trade show expenses. Not only that, they are the ones who actually use the product, so they know how it works and what it can do.

Most of Apple's booth is made up of developer demonstration stations. Developers work all the machines (they actually take turns and compete for how much time they get in the booth), so that the Regettes can schmooz with the press, Apple salespeople can do power lunches, and Apple product managers can attend Jean-Louis' keynote address to find out what they are supposed to be working on.

Booth Personnel

A glaring irony is that companies spend hundreds of thousands of dollars to build grand edifices, then they staff them with well-dressed nitwits. In 1984, the trade show booths of Macintosh companies were staffed by presidents and engineers. You could get an answer in those days.

By 1988, the situation had completely deteriorated, and trade show booths were staffed by professional rent-a-reps, clowns, magicians, and comedians. They are usually out-of-work actors, actresses, and models, and all they do is hand out chachkas[1] to attract crowds.

---

1. Chachkas are little valueless trinkets that companies give out at trade shows in order to insult your intelligence. Examples of chachkas are bags, pins, mugs, and mousepads. T-shirts (the cloth kind) are not chachkas; they are part of the development process.

Innovative Software set new lows for trade show appearances with the WingZ introductions. At the January, 1988 Macworld Expo in San Francisco, jump-suited "trekkies" gave you tote bags if you attended their Leonard Nimoy video. At the August, 1988 Macworld Expo in Boston jump-suited "trekkies" gave you tote bags (that broke after ten minutes of use) if you attended their Leonard Nimoy video. At the January, 1989 Macworld Expo in San Francisco it was the same thing again. They didn't have to do all that—WingZ is a great product.

Here's how to have the right personnel in your company's trade show booth:

1 ▶ Take the T-shirts. Take the T-shirts to trade shows to impress The Cult. T-shirts really know what they are talking about, and they are reassuring to prospective customers who visit your booth. T-shirts also make excellent scouts because they know how to embarrass the competition. I know when I'm in our trade show booth, I'm much more careful about what I say to a T-shirt than a Tie.

Exercise

Calculate the ratio of T-shirts to Mr. and Miss Americas in your booth.

---

2 ▶ Take your president. If your president isn't at the show, you'd better have an excellent reason why. Giving birth, a death in the family, or a plane crash are all acceptable. Super Bowl XXIII is not. What could be happening in the world that is more important for a Macintosh company than Macworld Expo? Charlie Jackson did every demo of SuperPaint for three days straight at the Dallas Macworld Expo in October, 1986.

3 ▶ Make sure your management is in the booth a lot. After a company gets to about the $5-million size, a strange thing starts to happen: management doesn't hang around the booth anymore. They are off meeting with analysts, schmoozing the press, or trying to sell the books that they wrote.

Trade shows are one of the few times that customers can meet your management, so make sure they are in the booth. Both may benefit. When Jim Young of EDS (the guy who's a charter member of the Apple Corps of Dallas) goes to Macworld Expo, he walks the floor of the show. You're not going to meet him in the press room or the speakers' lounge.

Booth Skills

Most companies think that trade shows are for MBAs and yellow ties to relate to other MBAs and yellow ties, so they don't train their booth staff. You should get your booth staff as ready as you can for The Cult. The best preparation is a role-playing exercise in which your technical support group plays trade show attendees. These are the right trade show skills:

1 ▶ Answer the question that's asked. A Cult friend of mine had this experience with Quark at the Seybold Desktop Publishing show. He found a T-shirt (actually, she was wearing a blouse and skirt) and asked her all of the questions he could think of. Later, he thought of another one so he went back to Quark's booth, but she was on a break so he asked a Miss America:

Friend: "Does QuarkXPress work with Coach Professional?"
Miss America: "QuarkXPress has an 80,000-word spelling checker."

Then he went to a yellow tie:
Friend: "Does QuarkXPress work with Coach Professional?"
Yellow tie: "QuarkXPress has an 80,000-word spelling checker."

He wanted to know about Coach Professional because he had built up a large dictionary over the past year. He decided to conduct an experiment: he asked every Quark employee in sight the same question to see if they all gave the same answer.

No one knew the answer, but everyone instantly knew the pat answer they were supposed to give. This isn't the way to prepare your staff. You can fool most of the people most of the time, but a great company doesn't even try.

Exercise
Call Quark (in Denver, Colorado) and ask them if XPress works with Coach Professional.

2 ▶ Concentrate on one person at a time. When someone asks you a question, pay full attention. It is distracting and impolite to look around, beyond, or through the person who's got you. Learn to hose people off quickly if you have to, but give them your full attention until you do. One good way to hose people off is to ask for their business card to "get back to them later."

3 ▶ Don't condescend. Any question asked in earnest is not a dumb question, and no one likes to do business with someone who makes them feel stupid. Therefore, never adopt a condescending attitude in your booth. Smaller, technically-oriented companies often do this because they only want to sell to technically-oriented people. Remember, money is money.

Getting the Most out of Trade Shows

So far this chapter has been about exhibiting at trade shows. Now I'd like to spend some time on attending trade shows. It comes down to a simple set of six rules:

1 ▶ Dress comfortably. There is absolutely no reason to dress up for a trade show. Don't ever forget that you are the customer and the companies want to sell to you. They know that jeans-and-t-shirt money is as good as three-piece-suit money. If they don't, you probably don't want their products anyway.

2 ▶ Go to the booths that have the company presidents. The presence of the company president in a trade show booth is one of the best indicators of the quality of the company and its products. The first thing you should ask in a booth is, "Is the president of your company here?" If he is, you've probably found a Macintosh Way company. If he is demoing the product, buy one.

3 ► Ask the right questions. These are the five most revealing questions (other than whether the president is in the booth) that you can ask the trade show personnel of a company:

▷   Can I try using your product in the booth?
▷   Are there any tech support engineers in the booth?
▷   Are any of the programmers in the booth?
▷   Are any of your outside developers or consultants in the booth?
▷   Can I get a demo version of your product?

4 ► Don't go to booths with entertainment. Booths that have actors performing skits, dancing gals and guys, and rock videos have something to hide. Either they don't have a good product or they don't have good booth personnel. The purpose of a trade show is informing, not entertaining. The only good thing about these booths is that you can rest your feet in them. Also, avoid booths with people in tuxedos and evening gowns. Aloha shirts are okay.

5 ► Avoid the large panels with vendor pukes. Most of these kinds of panels and seminars are moderated by people who know nothing about the subject and are filled with vendor pukes who only want to push their products. In the best case, you may see a few competitors tear each other's throats out. In the most likely case, you'll hear an hour of sales pitch superlatives.

6 ► Go to all the parties. The gala events that companies stage at trade shows are ridiculous displays of party envy. The philosophy behind them is: "We're so successful, we can spend $150,000 feeding and entertaining the trade show staff of our competitors."

You should always go to these parties because it's your money that they are wasting. Don't worry if the parties are supposed to be "by invitation only"; you can always get in with a good story. Nobody wants a scene at the door. Tell them you know me.

Exercise

One Macintosh software company threw a Macworld Expo party and spent $150,000 on roast beef, shrimp, chocolate desserts, an open bar, and famous entertainers to impress its competitors.

Another Macintosh software company bought a Testarossa for a company car and didn't throw a party. The day after the party, the first company was left with a dirty room and leftover food. The other company still had the Testarossa and all its employees enjoyed driving it. And it's still impressing its competitors.

Which is the smarter company?

How to Drive Your (MS-DOS) Competitors Crazy

If you would like to know what the Lord God thinks of money, you only have to look at those to whom he gives it.

Maurice Baring

The Good Ole Days

Dave Winer, the founder of Living Videotext, and I often reminisce about the early days of Macintosh. It's a beautiful pond. The water is crystal clear. The air is clean. Birds are singing. Then we open our eyes. The pond is polluted. MS-DOS companies are doing Macintosh software. Now that the fast is over, they want to join the banquet.

This chapter not only explains the right way to drive your competitors crazy; it also legitimizes the process. It's tailored to Macintosh developers, but these techniques are applicable to competition in any high-technology field.

MS-DOS companies think Macintosh companies are a bunch of rag-tag, product-crazed nuts anyway. Macintosh companies think of MS-DOS companies the way Oregonians think of Californians—"a bunch of bourgeois polluters." Vicious attacks are okay as long as they are witty and original, not heavy-handed and mundane.

A Macintosh programmer walked into a redneck bar in White Plains, New York. He went up to the bar, ordered a beer, and asked the bartender if he wanted to hear a joke about an MS-DOS programmer.

The bartender said, "I'm an MS-DOS programmer, and you see those two big guys shooting pool? They're MS-DOS programmers. Those guys arm wrestling? They're MS-DOS programmers, too."

The Macintosh programmer looked at all of them and said to the bartender, "I see your point. I guess I'd have to explain the joke too many times."

The Macintosh programmer bumped into two MS-DOS marketing executives in the parking lot as he was leaving. One of the marketeers had bought a new BMW and was having trouble with the rear turn signal. He asked the other marketeer to go behind the car and tell him if the turn signal was working. The marketeer went behind the car to look. "Is it working?" asked the first marketeer.

"Yes." "No." "Yes." "No," replied the marketeer behind the car.

Exercise

Free associate with the terms below. Compare your responses to the Macintosh and MS-DOS columns.

Term	Macintosh	MS-DOS
Raw Fish	Sushi	Bait
Evangelist	Prototypes	Sex
Customer	Make	Buy
Pundit	Alsop[1]	Dyson
Mouse	Input device	Hair gel
Display	Black on white	White on black
Startup	Inits	CONFIG.SYS

---

1. Stewart has quite a few MS-DOS types fooled into thinking he's a pundit too.

Mess Up Their Minds

MS-DOS companies think they are going to waltz into the Macintosh market—create an ordinary product, put on a yellow tie, slick on some mousse, slap on a suit—and it's a slam dunk, no brainer. Here's how to turn the palefaces into red faces. Welcome to Oregon—hope you enjoy your visit. Don't stay too long.

Step 1: Ruin their relationship with Apple.

MS-DOS companies think that Apple is the key to success in the Macintosh market. To them customers are merely victims of marketing campaigns. Therefore, step one is to ruin their relationship with Apple.

1 ▶ Make them think you're in so tight with Apple that your skivvies are six colors. Tell your competitor, "I was on my way to breakfast with Jean-Louis when Randy Battat (Apple's vice-president of product marketing) called me to find out if I got the new Macintosh prototype that Alan Kay showed me at John Sculley's birthday party the day after I had lunch with Allan Loren."

Exercise

Learn the correct pronunciation of Gassée (gass-SAY). Learn the correct spelling of "Sculley" (it has an "e"). Also, "Jobs" rhymes with "robs."

---

2 ▶ Tell them that Apple is funding a competitor. No one can figure out what the Apple venture capital group is doing, so use this to your advantage. For example, if you're with Oracle people, ask, "Did you know that Apple is investing more money in Sybase[1] in order to incorporate their technology into system software?"

---

1. Oracle and Sybase are two mainframe database companies who recently discovered Macintosh. They are named after two Greek gods who were banished from heaven by Zeus because they were always trying to kill each other. Now one lives in Belmont and one in Emeryville.

3 ▶ Harp on the Apple/Claris connection. Tell your competitor, "I hear that Claris is developing a product that competes with yours. Apple says that Claris is independent, but that's such a farce. Apple owns 85 percent of Claris. What an unfair advantage." The phone lines will burn.

4 ▶ Educate Apple. Apple wants to sell more Macintoshes. If the MS-DOS competitor sells a ported product, make a public statement that people should buy an AT clone, the company's MS-DOS product, and save their money instead. This will make Apple crazy. Thus endeth the co-marketing relationship.

Step 2: Befriend them.
After you've thoroughly ruined their mothership connection, you can focus directly on the competitor by using more samurai-like techniques.

1 ▶ Become their customer. Becoming the customer of your competitor enables you to see how they treat their installed base. The areas to study are support, upgrades, training, promotions, and developer programs. You can learn a lot about your competition without asking.

2 ▶ Be nice to their sales reps. Show them all of the cool technical tricks. Install F-keys and Inits. Zap parameter RAM. Rebuild the Desktop. Tell them that real Macintosh people use " " not " ". Show them how little they really know.

3 ▶ Help them penetrate the market. An MS-DOS software company called dBFast in Issaquah, Washington created a high-performance dBASE clone that runs on Macintosh. I told the president of dBFast, Phil Mickelson, that I wanted to create confusion in the dBASE clone Macintosh market and offered to help him.

My goal was to help dBFast create confusion about which Macintosh dBASE clone was the best, and let Fox, Nantucket, and dBFast beat each other's brains out. I sent Phil information about the Macintosh market, a copy of TopGuys (the 4th Dimension database of the best Macintosh contacts), and a database of Macintosh user groups.

4 ▶ Help their headhunters. Headhunters will often call you looking for candidates to fill positions at MS-DOS companies trying to enter the Macintosh market. When the headhunters call, give them the names of lousy employees at MS-DOS companies. This saddles the company that is gaining the employee with garbage, and destabilizes the company that is losing the employee.

Exercise

When an employee leaves one MS-DOS company to go to work for another MS-DOS company, the average IQ...

A. *Rises for the company that is losing the person.*

B. *Rises for the company that is gaining the person.*

C. *Rises for both companies.*

You can also give headhunters the names of good employees at MS-DOS companies. Anything that destabilizes the competition is good. This works very well when the headhunter is working for Apple because Apple can outbid anyone. When headhunters call you with candidates they are trying to place, keep the great ones, send the good ones to your friends, and send the losers to your competitors.

5 ▶ Encourage them to demo at user groups under MultiFinder and a prerelease System. If they don't crash when using MultiFinder and a prerelease System (or even more dangerous, a released System), they'll demo pure ignorance of Macintosh and get lynched. "We invented drop-down menus, you know," Hmm, "drop down"—that's what you expected Apple stock to do when OS/2 was shipped, right?

Step 3: Harass them

These techniques are not for amateurs or for use at home. They are industrial-strength techniques for untrained professionals. They may not accomplish anything except make you feel good.

1 ▶ Take on their management. In the Borland booth of the January 1988 Macworld Expo, Philippe Kahn bet me a trip and dinner in Paris that Reflex Plus could import data from "any database."

The Reflex Plus product manager, Laurie Flesher, and a tech support engineer were unable to import a 4th Dimension text file without altering the data, and they used 4th Dimension to do that. I almost made reservations at the Crillon (not even Jean-Louis stays in this hotel because it's so expensive) the next day.

Did I collect? Of course not. Philippe's excuse was that 4th Dimension could do things that Reflex Plus couldn't because it was a bigger program. That wasn't the bet. What do you expect of someone who thinks that Macintosh is "a piece of sheet?"

Exercise

Match the quote to the speaker.

Macintosh is a strategic   *Jim Manzi,*
part of our business.   *Lotus Development*

Macintosh is a strategic   *Philippe Kahn,*
part of our business.   *Borland International*

Macintosh is a strategic   *Fred Gibbons,*
part of our business.   *Software Publishing*
                                     Corporation

Bonus Points:
When did Manzi, Kahn, and Gibbons say this?

A. 1983–1989

B. 1983–1989

C. 1983–1989

---

2 ▶ Position their products as ports. MS-DOS companies think that inter-operability[1] is a strength. They don't understand that port is a four-letter word to a Macintosh fanatic. Port is a wine—not a development path.

Exercise

Go to a liquor store and buy the cheapest port you can find. Drink some.

---

1. Inter-operability is the ability of a software product to run on more than one brand of computer. Many analysts think that having products that run on more than one brand of computer is good because it enables you to raise more venture capital.

3 ▶ Charge more for your product than they do. MS-DOS companies think that customers buy from them because of their big name, solidity, and reputation for support. When a punk Macintosh start-up charges more than they do, their noses start bleeding.

4 ▶ Scramble them. I used to send the Ashton-Tate dBASE Mac product manager, Dan Goldman, mailings that looked like they were going to all our customers. Once I sent him an ACIUS mug with a cover letter that started like this:

Dear Customer:
Our first year has been a phenomenal success so we wanted to thank you by sending you an ACIUS mug.

I also sent him a similar letter with an ACIUS t-shirt. I wanted him to think that ACIUS was so successful and service-oriented that our customers were getting these gifts in the normal course of events.

Exercise

> *If the enemy general is obstinate and*
> *prone to anger, insult and enrage him, so*
> *that he will be irritated and confused,*
> *and without a plan will recklessly ad-*
> *vance against you.*
>
> *The Art of War*
> Sun Tzu

Buy a Porsche (at least a 911) on the day that your competitor ships a new product. It might insult and enrage him. If not, you still have a hot car. Better yet, buy an Acura so that your competitor will know how smart you are.

Microsoft

One Time Offer: Send us the title page of your manual and $5 and we will send you version 3.0 of the same application. Type of software doesn't matter—we want it all. End users only, please. Megalosoft. Renton, Washington.

**Classified ad in the
1987 April Fools issue
of *Outside Apple***

Microsoft is a glaring and unique exception to MS-DOS bozosity in the Macintosh market. Microsoft is an awesome company, and we can all learn from it. Here's why Microsoft is so great:

1 ▶ Bill Gates is a tweak. He has the best understanding of technology of any software company president; the proof is that he jumped on Macintosh development in 1982.

2 ▶ Bill Gates considers everyone to be the enemy. He will kill anyone who gets in his way—not only big companies like Ashton-Tate but small companies like T/Maker. To ruin the market for T/Maker's word processor, Microsoft sold inexpensive upgrades to an upcoming version of Word when T/Maker was about to ship their product.

Exercise

Put your head in a vise. Squeeze it as tight as you can stand. This is what it's like to compete with Microsoft.

3 ▶ Bill Gates has incredible chutzpah. He tells Apple how high to jump. I know, I've seen him in action. He must have taken steroids. Somehow they affected his personality but not his physique. He's still afraid of BMUG, though.

Microsoft deserves its success. It jumped on Macintosh development early, it's a tough competitor, and it has great products. Still, I'd love to see someone knock it off the pedestal.

A Parting Request

It's fun to drive your competition crazy. I think it's almost your moral duty. If you can think of any more ways, please be sure to contact me because this is one of my favorite subjects.

The Macintosh Guide to Dating and Marriage

Behind every successful man there stands an amazed woman.
Anonymous

In case you read this book and you don't run a company, here's a real-life application of the Macintosh Way. This chapter explains the Macintosh Way of dating and marriage.[1]

Beth and I did the *MacWEEK* ad on the next page because it was fun and because we admire *MacWEEK* for its fearlessness. We wanted the headline to read, "Only two things really excite my husband, and he gets one of them only once a week," but *MacWEEK* wimped out. Maybe they aren't so fearless after all.

High-Tech Dating (For Men)

There are six good women for every good man in high technology, so I will concentrate on helping more men break into the "good" range. Frankly, it will do men more good because men need more help. This is the right way to date (for men).

1 ▶ Position yourself as a tool. High-tech women are not masochists—they have careers that are as interesting and

---

1. The people who read drafts of this book were split almost exactly 50/50 on this chapter. Half said that I should take it out because it has little to do with running a business. Half said it was the best chapter of the book. I left it in—after all, this is my book.

Guy Kawasaki won't tell us what comes in second, but he admits that MacWEEK ranks at the top of his list.

"I'm scared if ACIUS is mentioned and I'm scared if it's not," confides the vigilant Kawasaki, who knows how much impact a MacWEEK mention can have on an ACIUS product — or one of its competitors.

He reads MacWEEK cover to cover every week because it's the only magazine that keeps pace with the accelerating momentum of the Macintosh marketplace.

"MacWEEK has great sources," says Kawasaki, who appreciates MacWEEK's aggressive reporting, critical reviews and valuable insider information.

Dependably delivered to Kawasaki and 50,000 other influential Mac professionals every week, MacWEEK is definitely something to get exited about.

"Only two things really excite my husband."

Beth Kawasaki
Wife of ACIUS' President
Guy Kawasaki

important as yours. To be attractive in this kind of market, you have to be a tool, not a problem. Do something useful like checking her hard disk for viruses (but not on the first date) or debugging her 100,000-line assembly language program.

2 ▸ Treat your date like she is the only platform in the world. Put this on your floppy disk and write-protect it because this is the key to successful dating. The Joe Isuzu dating paradigm— Italian suits, leased teutonic wagons, cellular phones, and

IPOs—do not equal kindness and attention as user-friendly features. Inter-operability is not a desired feature in dating.

Exercise
Rent a Ford Escort. Ask the most desirable woman you know for a date.[1] Try to impress her.

3 ▸ Maintain an open architecture. An open system is as important for dating as it is for personal computers. Possessiveness too early is a big mistake, so don't close the system until the proper, mutually satisfying configuration is reached. It's not like software—don't announce, then ship, then test. Instead, go alpha, then beta, then golden. You may be living with this release a lot longer than with your software.

4 ▸ Form strategic alliances. It's puzzling that men who spend all day forming, preannouncing, and announcing strategic alliances cannot apply the same techniques to their social lives. Strategic alliances with friends, roommates, and family can make or break you in high-tech dating.

Friends and roommates are likely to shape a woman's initial opinion of you. They probably know all her old boyfriends and are comparing you from the first moment you meet.

Also, when you get serious, it's not with a person but a family. It's easier to sell The Macintosh Office without a fileserver than date successfully without parental approval.

5 ▸ Never ignore your installed base. No matter how good things are going, never ignore your installed base (i.e., your old girlfriends). They can provide advice, add mystery and challenge if someone is taking you for granted, and introduce you to more women.

---

1. Dating is when two people go someplace where there are no computers, talk about anything except computers, and do analog stuff afterward.

6 ▸ Here are some final tips for Macintosh men. Put them in ROM[1] and solder in the chip:

▷ Always believe it's your privilege and honor to be with your date.
▷ Never be late.
▷ Aspire to be best friends.
▷ Don't be afraid to show weakness.
▷ Never criticize your date in public.
▷ Never compare your date unfavorably to anyone except her mother.

High-Tech Dating (For Women)

Well, honey, let's face the sad news: the odds are against you. There are very few men worth competing for (and many good women you are competing with) so you have to do what's necessary to date high-tech men.

1 ▸ Make yourself more physically attractive. When it comes to women, men, all men, especially high-tech men, can see better than they can think. Sad commentary but true. High-

1. ROM stands for Read-Only Memory. That's the place in a computer that doesn't go away when you shut off the power. It's also the place where computer companies put their worst idiosyncrasies.

tech men are body by Volkswagen, brains by Cray, heart by Frigidaire, personality by Metamucil. And all men are SCSIs.[1]

2 ▸ Hang around high-tech joints. If you want to meet high-tech men, you've got to hang around high-tech joints like Fry's Electronics[2] or Comdex.[3] I never said it would be easy or pleasant. Try to get to Fry's around dusk so you can see the nerds watching the sun set over the Santa Cruz mountains.

3 ▸ Take the first step. Most high-tech men are as sophisticated as the UNIX interface when it comes to taking the first step, so you are going to have to take the initiative. Unplug the AppleTalk cable from the LaserWriter and then hang around until they show up trying to figure out what went wrong. Shutting down the AppleShare fileserver would work too. Do something. Anything.

Exercise

Which opening line do you think would work best with a Macintosh man?

A. Would you unzap my parameter RAM?

B. Haven't I seen your Navigator face file before?

C. What's your file type and creator, handsome?

D. Want to see my PICT files sometime?

E. My disk is fragmented. Do you know where I can get SUM?

---

1. SCSI stands for Small Computer System Interface. It is the name of the type of port or orifice on Macintoshes. Thus, "all men are SCSIs" is an adaptation of a frequently heard phrase when single women get together.

2. Fry's Electronics is the ultimate nerd store in Silicon Valley. At Fry's you can buy Jolt, DRAMS, chips (both the kind you plug in and get fat on), and CDs all in one place.

3. Comdex is a computer show that is held in Atlanta and Las Vegas each year. It is supposed to be for retailers to see upcoming new products. In reality, it's just a bunch of employees from hard disk manufacturers who go to each other's booths to look at the latest in platters.

4 ► Get it up front. Don't put up with a vesting period. A good rule of thumb for engagement rings is one carat of diamond per computer. My wife says that a LaserWriter counts as a computer because it has a 68000[1] in it.

DINC[2] to SINC

Somehow a woman married me, so this advice must work. Being married, however, definitely affects your career path. When I first thought of starting a company, I asked my wife Beth if she would still love me if I left Apple (and its salary, options, and profit sharing).[3] Her reply was, "Of course I'll still love you. I'll also miss you."

I've found that what made you fascinating to date can make you "shallow" and "narrow-minded" after you're married. When I was dating my wife, she thought it was the coolest thing that I was a big deal in the Macintosh community. Now, she'd like to take a sword to my—I mean our—poor Macintosh.

Beth and I have been married for over three years now, and I believe that getting and staying married rounds out and balances your life. She worked at Apple in the Seattle office and then in Cupertino, so she's been infected by Macintosh too. Recently she quit Apple to do what she really wants—design clothes—and we went from DINC to SINC.

Working at Home—Beth 1, Guy 0

Working at home is productive because you're not interrupted by phone calls, meetings, and other distractions. I do my best work at home alone in the solitude of Macintosh bliss.

Unfortunately, spouses believe that time at home should be shared. The key to being able to work at home is to con-

---

1. A 68000 is the name of the Motorola chip that is the brains of a Macintosh. 68000s have broken up more marriages than affairs, drugs, and fast cars combined.

2. Double Income No Clones.

3. Profit sharing is what's left after paying for the senior executive bonuses, the leased Mercedes, the fresh orange juice, the first class flights, and the Bösendorfer grands.

vince your spouse that by working extra hard your company will achieve success sooner and you can vacation more and retire earlier. If you figure out the right way to do this, I'd appreciate hearing from you.

Exercise

A woman started a company. She worked long hours and traveled a lot. After a year, the company was successful, and the woman came home earlier, didn't bring work home, and was generally attentive. She and her husband live in Portola Valley, they have two beautiful kids, and they vacation at the Mauna Lani four weeks each summer.

The best title for this passage is:

A. *The World According to Kleiner-Perkins*

B. *Yeah, Right.*

C. *Mauna Lani Customer Profile*

D. *The Long Term Effects of Reality Distortion*

E. *If You Lose Your Dream You Die*

There are three additional techniques that you can use to slide past your spouse. First, pay a little attention to your spouse before you start working. A little bit of attention—a kiss, a hug—when you enter your home can add a few hours to Mac time. I try to wait at least 60 seconds before I get on my Macintosh.

Secondly, try to incorporate some of your spouse's interests in your conversation. Because my wife is interested in fashion design I try to talk about the implications of Display

PostScript[1] on her field. This doesn't work quite right.

Thirdly, convince your spouse that you are creating art, not working or playing on your Macintosh. My wife let me work on this book (and therefore my Macintosh) for many hours because I told her that "I'm writing, not working on my Macintosh"—à la Ernest Hemingway, J.D. Salinger, or Colette. This works all right for a while.

CompuServe—Beth 2, Guy 0

CompuServe and the four other electronic bulletin boards that I belong to drive my wife nuts. She can't understand how I can spend so much time E-mailing total strangers. She especially can't deal with how amusing I find Navigator[2] face files.[3]

Jonathan Goldman   Deirdre L. Maloy   John Kirkilis

The 2400-baud line for CompuServe requires a message unit call where we live. One month we had a $200 message unit bill. Mind you, this was not the CompuServe bill (I have a free account), this was the phone bill. I'm no dummy; now I use a toll-free number so she can't see how often I sign on.

Exercise

Send me an EasyPlex on CompuServe. My account is 76703,3031. Ask me if Beth wants me off the computer.

---

1. Display PostScript is a graphics language developed by Adobe Systems. Apple is so upset about the royalties it pays Adobe for PostScript in its printers that it refuses to adopt Display PostScript for its displays.

2. Navigator is a program that makes access to CompuServe easier. It should have reduced people's connect time to CompuServe, but it has had the exact opposite effect. Now people connect more often and longer because it is easier. I don't think CompuServe planned it this way, but it's better to be rich than smart.

3. Face files are pictures of the sender and recipient of messages on CompuServe so that everyone has an idea of what the people look like. Clever people even make the lips of the faces move.

This leads me to explain the right way to get on and stay on CompuServe and other electronic bulletin boards:

▷ Get a separate data line[1] so you don't fight for the phone.
▷ Turn off the modem speaker so she can't hear you connect.
▷ Have the phone bill go to the office.
▷ Have the CompuServe bill go to the office.
▷ Use software that autoconnects at preset times.

Business Travel—Beth 3, Guy 0

My wife hates it when I go away on business. If you've ever seen me speak at a user group, you know I arrive in the afternoon and fly out the same evening. I bet you thought it was because I had some important business meeting to attend.

At first, my wife used to come with me on business trips so that we could travel together. That didn't last long because she didn't want to be around me when I'm with other Macintosh nerds. It seems that our conversations don't cover the full gamut of music, literature, and art.

I even tried to convince her that an August vacation in Boston would be fun. There are a lot of historical things to see in Boston, like the World Trade Center,[2] and we wouldn't have to bring any warm clothes. Now I bring her back a mousepad from every city I visit. She is somewhat less appreciative than one might hope.

So Who's Keeping Score?

We are not going to win this battle. I've come to the conclusion that the right thing to do is pay more attention to our spouses than our Macintoshes. That is, until we get our laptop Macintoshes...

---

1. This way she won't pick up the phone and have the modem carrier tone screaming in her ear and her friends won't tell her that the phone was busy for hours.

2. The World Trade Center is where the Boston Macworld Expo is held every August. Well, about half of the Boston Macworld Expo, anyway. The only thing worse than its location is its air conditioning.

Sayonara

There are two things to aim at in life: first, to get what you want, and after that to enjoy it. Only the wisest of mankind achieve the second.
Logan Pearsall Smith

It's hard to end this book because the Macintosh Way is still changing and growing. If you have any comments or ideas about the Macintosh Way, I'd love to hear from you. You can reach me in many ways:

AppleLink	Kawasaki2
MCI Mail	GKawasaki
CompuServe	76703,3031
FAX	(408) 252-0831
Telephone	(408) 252-4444 x 210
US Mail	10351 Bubb Road Cupertino, CA 95014

Exercise

Go out and buy a copy of 4th Dimension. See if you get a thank-you note from me.

Index

202

205

207

How This Book
Was Made

Guy created outlines for the book with Acta and MORE. Most of the writing was done using Microsoft Word on a Macintosh SE with Radius Full-Page Display and a Radius accelerator card. Drafts of the book were sent over MCI Mail using Desktop Express. QuickKeys was indispensable throughout.

Electronic art was created with Aldus FreeHand. The final layout was done in PageMaker from Aldus and output at Seattle Imagesetting on a Linotronic PostScript imagesetter. The type is set in the Stone Serif and Stone Sans typeface families, designed by Sumner Stone of Adobe Systems in the late 1980s.